How to Live to Be
— 100 —
and Like It!

A Handbook for the Newly Retired

C LIFFORD B EBELL

iUniverse, Inc.
Bloomington

How to Live to Be 100 and Like It!
A Handbook for the Newly Retired

iUniverse books may be ordered through booksellers or by contacting:

iUniverse
1663 Liberty Drive
Bloomington, IN 47403
www.iuniverse.com
1-800-Authors (1-800-288-4677)

ISBN: 978-1-4502-9334-1 (pbk)
ISBN: 978-1-4502-9335-8 (cloth)
ISBN: 978-1-4502-9336-5 (ebk)

Printed in the United States of America

iUniverse rev. date: 3/23/2011

Contents

Part 4   Later Days

Key Ideas

Introduction:
No! No! No! or Yes! Yes! Yes!
Which Is It?

So now you're 65!

Or almost.

And you're retired.

Or looking to retire—sooner than you'd like. (No! No! No!)

Unless you're one of those who can't wait—who's been counting the days. (Yes! Yes! Yes!)

The first of you can't imagine how he* will fill the days, while the second is sure retirement will be an endless round of fun and games—the 'Golden Years.'

You've long been told that you're about to enter these 'Golden Years.' Don't believe it! They <u>can</u> be golden, but you have to make them so. Furthermore, retirement is <u>not</u> all partying and vacationing. I once met a lady in Hawaii (originally from Wisconsin), who with her husband had "retired to Paradise" several years earlier. Both were almost climbing the walls, scrambling to find something to do.

---

*I'm not going to use clumsy phrases, like 'he (or she),' or 'she (or he)'—with or without parentheses—every time I refer to a person who could be of either sex. And especially I'm not going to use the often-ungrammatical 'they.' Nor am I going to employ the masculine form, and expect you to know that it might be a woman as well as a man. Instead, I'm going to alternate my usage between masculine and feminine, using the former in odd-numbered chapters, and the latter in even.

1

So, both the **No! No! No!** protester and the **Yes! Yes! Yes!** devotee are wrong. The first will find more demands on his time than he ever expected, while the latter will discover that he quickly tires of constant rounds of bridge, or golf, or whatever.

What both of you need to know is that retirement is <u>the rest of your life</u>. This is the way you'll live from now on. And if you want to live long and well—to get to be a happy, healthy 100, say—you'll need to make plans and develop habits to help you succeed. The purpose of this little volume is to suggest things to do and not do.

Retirement years are not easy. I think it was Bette Davis who said, "Old age is not for sissies." You bet! Further, it's all new territory. Even though you're still the same person you always were, the circumstances of being a senior are different from those of earlier years, and the adjustments you'll make are markedly different from those of previous times—when you may have had to deal with children, mortgages, job changes, residence moves, and endless chores.

You'll have to cope with a life change almost as traumatic as your original birth (some 65 years past, more or less)—or the onset of your adolescence so long ago (remember that?), Many of the people, places, activities, and habits of your past will change. You'll need to decide what you want to do, and how to plan your time—in short, who you're going to be from now on—creating life patterns to endure through old age.

And this is harder than you think. You may believe that a lifetime of acquiring skills, habits, and interests, has given you everything you need to adjust to any circumstance. Not so. Sitting on the sidelines, struggling to fill the calendar, making new decisions, dealing with unaccustomed aches and pains—these, and more, call for thought and effort. And don't forget that, at some point, you'll face declining capabilities.

Eventually, you'll almost come to feel as though you've been re-born. Your new world will include a shift in the ways people treat you—the things they say and do. There'll also be a shift in the things <u>you</u> do—not simply your reactions to them, and the addition of new leisure-time activities—but everything you spend time on, and the ways in which you organize your life. You'll make decisions and plans you haven't had to make before.

You may not believe me, After all, the first day after you retire you wake up the same person you were the day before. Your life seems changed only by the fact that you don't have to race through breakfast and scramble to work. You enjoy the thought that the rat race is finally over, and your life is your own at last. What could be better?

In fact a lot of things! But you'll have to make them so. I've called this book *How to Live to Be 100—and Like It* for a reason. The reason is that the steps you take in early retirement can determine how long, and how well you'll live. Your habits and attitudes from now on will have an ever-increasing impact on your health and longevity.

I think it was John D. Rockefeller who said, "I'm going to live to be 100, or die trying." This is my mantra. And I want to make it yours. Especially, I want the first part of John D.'s plan to be more likely for you than the second. As we often hear, old age is "Better than the alternative." I believe there's a way of dealing with life which increases your chances of reaching an advanced age. After you read this book, I hope you'll believe it, too. And If you follow the suggestions in it, you'll be living your retirement years to the maximum.

I hear you ask, "Who are you?" "Why are you qualified to offer advice?" I admit that I'm not a specialist in gerontology, or finance, or psychology. In fact, I was a teacher of mathematics, and later a professor of education most of my working life. But I've travelled many miles in your moccasins—and I've learned most of what I suggest the hard way. As I write these lines, I've passed my 94th birthday, I've been retired for over 30 years, and I feel my longevity means I must be doing something right—besides choosing the right father and mother in 1915. You who read these lines will have decide if I'm kidding myself.

I'll share the struggles I've had in coming to terms with advancing years. I'll try to draw on my experiences to help you look sensibly at your own conditions and problems—especially, the advice and pressures you'll get from family and friends. I shall not repeat the extensive information so widely disseminated about services available to seniors, and any legal, financial, or health advice I give is simply relayed from experts. There are so many lawyers, accountants, advisors, gerontologists, and other health professionals who offer this kind of help. What I shall do is look at how you might react to all of that

The book is divided into four parts, plus an intro and a finale. (I've also added an afterword, prepared after the book was fully written). The first section is called 'First Days,' although it might well have been entitled 'First Daze,' since it deals with what you learn and what you have to do early on, before you're really ready.

The second is called 'The Long Haul,' and it's about what you have to <u>do</u> and <u>be</u> in retirement, if you're planning to stick around for 35 years or more. It's meant to help you settle in during your active period, and be ready for later. This is the period you can make into your very own 'Golden Days.'

The third part is called 'The Home Stretch,' and the fourth, 'The End Zone.' The former deals with the time when you begin to make some concessions to the years, as you lose some strength and agility. The latter is concerned with your life beyond that, when more and more adjustments are necessary.

I give these two a lot of attention, although they may not affect you for some time. They represent new experiences for most retirees, and present problems you may not have thought about. But your success and happiness in these later stages depend heavily on the habits and attitudes you develop earlier, and the more you plan ahead for them. Of course, I have a great deal of interest in them for myself, as I approach the end of The Home Stretch.

Each chapter in the book (if indeed any is long enough to be called a chapter) is organized in the following way. I begin with a discussion of its theme, and follow with one or more lists of key ideas—mostly suggestions for your use. The lists are laid out in boldface, each on a separate page, so that the major ideas are easy to find later, if you wish to refer back to them.

The book is not long; yet I hope it's worth your time.

So, let's go!

What Is Retirement?

Retirement should not be thought of as retirement <u>from</u> something so much as retirement <u>to</u> something—the life you'll be leading from now on.

You will make many changes in your activities, your plans, your life style, and where you'll be living.

There may well be changes in your friendships, and in the persons you'll have regular contact with.

You'll spend less time on recreational activities than you anticipate, and more time on helping others.

You'll find yourself surprisingly busy with things you didn't expect to be so involved with.

Your family relationships will also change—perhaps in surprising ways.

You'll value many people and many activities differently than you did previously.

You'll probably work harder on your relationships with friends and family than before.

The First Day of the Rest of Your Life

It's hard to believe, but the first day after you retire is truly the first day of a new lifestyle, which will be the basis of your life for all your remaining years. You might call it—not your second childhood, but—your second adulthood.

The time you spend in retirement may well constitute the longest period of your life without major change.

You will see a progression of small changes—you may move from being an active householder to becoming a dweller in smaller quarters and/or new locations. You add and subtract activities as your interests and abilities change. Eventually, you reach a time when you are more and more restricted because of physical (and possibly, mental) limitations.

But each change will seem reasonable at the time, and usually each is anticipated well in advance, with little urgency involved. The whole process unrolls smoothly, usually without a sense of crisis.

In brief, retirement is the rest of your life, and should be viewed as a whole, with plans for finding the best way to deal with each aspect of it.

The thrust of this book is to look at the challenges you face in the various stages of this life, and to suggest ways of handling each in a manner that will leave you happy and contented.

This is emphasized because experience shows that overall planning is seldom done, with most retirees letting life happen as it comes along—often allowing other people to make decisions for them, especially in the later stages.

About This Book
Major Points

Retirement is <u>the rest of your life</u>, and should be planned for.

There are certain practices which will improve your life and increase your life span.

Adopting these will give you at least a fighting chance to reach 100.

Allowing yourself to drift is a shortcut to decline.

There are four stages of retirement—first shock, active years, long haul, end game.

The first is a time of adjustment.

The second is a time to make your new self.

The third is a time of declining capabilities.

The fourth is a time to be faced with courage.

I've lived through the first two, and am well into the third—I've learned much, and want to share what I've learned.

The Key Ideas

There are 116 lists of key ideas scattered throughout the book, each of them following a chapter discussing a major area related to life after retirement, and presenting thoughts relevant to it.

The purpose of these ideas is to give you, the reader, something concrete to think about.

My hope, however, is to go further than merely cause you to think; instead, my efforts are meant to encourage you to try applying the ideas in practice.

Of course, all efforts to persuade others fail, at least in part; any writer finds that not every thought he advances is appealing to everyone, and some perhaps not even to anyone, so it would be foolish for me to think that I am an exception.

At the same time, most of the ideas have resulted from my own life experiences, and I feel that many of them have held up well in the real world.

I've tried to make the proposals as clear and practical as possible, and to do my best to be persuasive.

All I ask is that you read them with an open mind, think about them, and use what appeals to you.

If any of them prove useful, I'll feel that my efforts have been worthwhile.

PART 1
– *First Days* –

First Daze?

I've already laid out the organization of this book. Now I'll outline the contents of Part 1.

This deals with the period immediately following retirement, when you're faced with many decisions and many changes. As I said above, I was tempted to call it "First Daze.," because the multitude of these can be overwhelming.

The main areas include:

1) How people look at you differently and what to do about it;

2) How you adapt and change;

3) What your new lifestyle will be like;

4) The major decisions you'll have to make:
   What to do about health,
   Where to live,
   How to pay for it all.

These are the main issues which arise during the early years of retirement, when you're still strong and vigorous, and can go anywhere and do anything you like (at least, that you can afford).

It may come as a surprise to find that the first days tin which you're able to do exactly what you want to do are co-opted by urgencies. You may find yourself unprepared to make hard choices. But you have to, and this part of the book is dedicated to helping it happen successfully.

The rest of the book concerns matters which will arise later. However, they should be of interest to you from the beginning because the decisions you make and the habits you establish at this time will have a major impact over the years, and will go a long way to determine how long you'll live.

CHAPTER 1

Your New Image

Who, Me?

One of the first things you'll notice after you retire, and perhaps the biggest surprise, is how differently others perceive you. Many will feel you've changed from being a productive member of society to one who sits on the sidelines. No longer a contributor, you now benefit from the contributions of others.

Also, you've lost the identity you had from your job. You may not realize how much you used your job to define yourself. until you have the task of doing it without saying, "I work for the XYZ Company," or "I'm in construction" or "I'm with the Post Office, or the school system," or whatever. This is why you often hear older people talk about what they did during their working lives, until their story gets old. People like to use a job as a means to describe or refer to a person, and this is now gone for you,

Then, there's the growing belief that you are now one of the seniors whose interests may be at variance with those of the rest of society. You're probably now a member of AARP (American Association of Retired Persons—as if you didn't know), if for no other reason than the discounts and special services. But, the AARP is often seen by employed citizens as a fearsome power in Washington that's pushing all kinds of special benefits and privileges—benefits and privileges workers have to pay for. Whether you're an AARP member or not, you're tarred with this brush, and there's little you can do about it.

Medicare is also seen as a special benefit others are underwriting, and you'll be both envied and resented by those who are either without health insurance, or struggling mightily to pay for it.

Social security is another issue. You've heard the dire predictions. Presumably, the ratio of working people to those who are retired is on a steady decline, with the result that fewer and fewer wage earners will be supporting each retiree. You've been told that eventually the system will reach a point where benefits will either be drastically reduced, or available only at a later age, or both. Inevitably, many workers think present retirees have it better than they will, and this may affect their attitude toward you.

So, you'll be both envied and resented. You'll be envied for your presumed life style—full of leisure and recreation. Those who count the years, months, and days till retirement may envy you at the same time that they marginalize you. They see you as already living in a special world, where you don't have to go to work, can stay home and goof off all day— entertaining yourself endlessly. They both lust for this and disrespect it.

It's a little frustrating to learn that your views are no longer considered to be as valid as they once were. People who are still active members of the "real" world tend to view those who are not as somehow less well-informed, and less able to do things than they are. Not only that, they often consider retirees to represent a special interest that's at least questionable.

No matter how courteous people are, if they are of this opinion, they'll show it in various little ways. They may pay less attention to you than to others, they may be dismissive of your suggestions and thoughts, they may spend less time with you than formerly, or they may no longer accept your offers to help. Since they believe you're out of things, and will continue to be—to an ever-increasing degree—your opinion is less often sought or followed. You're no longer on the inside.

This circumstance will exist for the rest of your life, so you have to come to terms with it. It helps if you understand why people act the way they do. In addition to points made above, it's possibly a manifestation of a need they have to feel valuable and competent. They sometimes do this by comparing their circumstances with those of others, and feel reassured if theirs are superior.

Also, there's a widespread tendency to hope someone in a privileged state has shortcomings—a thought which helps them feel better about it. This of course explains much of the prejudice and rejection which exist in the world—the bigotry and bias, the racism, the sexism, the xenophobia, the religious hatreds. It explains ageism, which may be a part of the view workers take of retirees. The tendency to compare one's situation with that of others is nearly universal, and unless it occurs in extreme form, probably does little harm.

So, the changed image which you now project is not a serious problem—if you don't let it be. The behavior I describe is not generally intentional. No one is consciously trying to marginalize you. Whatever is said or done can easily be ignored, unless you carry a chip on your shoulder. You should have more important things to do.

I've discovered that if I understand the motivations of others, I find myself having a greater wish to help them than resent them. And in trying to be supportive of their needs and feelings, I often lose sight off my own problems. Friends and family members who may unconsciously put you down also care about you. Most of the time you can enjoy the positive aspects of contact with them, and ignore anything else.

As I've said, you've entered a new universe, and will have to come to terms with it. In the lists that follow, I suggest things you can and can't say, and things you can and can't do. I've also added a few of the peeves I've accumulated over the years, as I've travelled the road you're entering upon. I hope you'll be encouraged to make lists of your own.

In later chapters I discuss the decisions you'll have to make, the problems and conditions you'll confront, both now and later, and ways to proceed if you're going to live to be 100.

What Am I—Chopped Liver?
Ways in which you are seen differently

Please forgive the New York slang (I was born there), but sometimes your irritation at being characterized or put down makes you want to say something angry.

Things people may say:

"We're not doing it that way any more."

"The new man in your job has really brought in some great new ideas."

"Boy, do you ever have it easy!"

"What do you do with all your time?"

"Gee, you're lucky to be getting all those senior discounts."

"I think you members of AARP are asking too much."

"Please understand—we need new blood on the Board this year."

"The point you made was considered some time ago."

"Let me go over these instructions again."

"Why don't you take things a little easier from now on."

"You shouldn't be lifting that box."

"Don't try to climb that ladder!"

Things You Can't Say

Interference & Unwanted Advice

"We tried that same approach back in 19-blankety blank—it didn't work"

"<u>This</u> is how we used to do it."

"Let me tell you (or show you) how to fix that."

"You can't get there if you turn here."

Unpleasant Assertions & Complaints

"I told you so!"

"Medicare should have covered this."

"Why isn't Social Security enough to live on?"

"Why do you like that contraption?"

Excess Nostalgia

"When I was your age....."

"Kids are not so well-behaved (or whatever) these days."

"The entertainment we used to have was so much better."

"My parents brought me up the right way."

Resistance

"I don't need your suggestions."

"Don't tell <u>me</u> what to do (or how to do it)."

"I've been cooking (or whatever) since you were in diapers."

"You've told me this too many times already."

Things You Can Say

Willingness to Listen

"Please help me decide what I should do."

"Please teach me to use the computer (or the cell phone, or whatever)."

"Explain this new health law to me."

"Should we re-think my life insurance?"

Appreciation of Help

"I can't thank you enough for all the help you've given me."

"You've done a great job with the kids (or the house, or whatever)."

"I don't know how I'd get along without you."

"You're so busy—how do you do it all?"

Sturdy Self-Reliance

"I'm getting along very well."

"I feel just fine!"

"I think I'm very lucky."

"I really need to do this for myself."

Efforts to be helpful in your turn

"Let me take care of the children tonight."

"Is there something I can do while you're gone?"

"I'd like to help with the family get-together."

"Use my car if you need to."

Things Not To Do

DON'T—

Monopolize the conversation.

Talk incessantly about the past.

Let your health problems dominate a friendly talk.

Dwell on a single topic over and over.

Complain!!!

Interfere in your children's lives (let them be independent)

Give unsolicited advice.

Expect too much time, attention, and service from family members.

Criticize your treatment by family, friends, care-givers or others— to outsiders, or to those who cannot do anything about it.

Be stubbornly determined to prove that you can do anything you used to be able to do.

Watch television, or play video games, long hours every day.

Travel alone, unless you've talked it over with someone whose judgment you trust.

Things To Do

Everything below is suggested somewhere else in this book—at greater length, and with supporting material. They are listed here as a summation of ideas I consider especially important.

DO—

Everything you possibly can for yourself.

Walk, walk, walk—every day.

Exercise your mind every day.

Your share, when tasks are being assigned.

Be a friend to lonely people.

Ask people about their interests and activities, and be admiring and encouraging.

In a conversation, really listen to what other people are saying, without simply waiting to put in your own comments.

Share in group activities.

Something outside your living quarters every day—whenever the weather permits.

Keep up with the news—TV, newspaper, news magazine, or internet.

My Pet Peeves

(Things you may have to put up with—
but which may not bother you)

Young people who call me by my first name, without asking if I mind—the younger, the more irritating.

Being grabbed by the arm, and "helped," without being asked if I need help.

Being called "old man," as in "Don't do that, old man."

Being told, "Things are different now," every time I express an opinion.

People talking to me too slowly or too loudly, as if I were not capable of understanding otherwise.

Persons in a group or meeting who ignore my effort to participate, or who show exasperation at having to listen to my comments.

The assumption that there's nothing I can do, when tasks are being handed out.

Childproof caps on pill bottles—which are often senior-proof, too. (Sometimes, you ask the kids to open them.)

Being put in the worst seat or the worst table, seemingly automatically.

When arrangements are made in consultation with everyone else except me.

Chapter 2

Your New You

Yes, You!

How can there be a new you after you retire? Aren't you still the same person—probably living in the same house, sleeping in the same bed, and with the same family and friends?

Will you change after you retire?

Will your behavior change?

The answer to both these questions is, Yes. Now we'll discuss some of the ways this might happen.

In the previous chapter I spoke of what you can and can't say and do. Now I consider how all this affects you. If you're being perceived differently by others, you inevitably have some reaction to their attitudes. This is not to say that you do what they expect. But it does mean that you become aware of how they see you, and this can shape your behavior and your outlook. Certainly, one thing you'll do is decide how to treat those who condescend to you.

You'll be affected in other ways, too. For example, having the whole day to use as you see fit is a major life alteration. How do you handle it? You can laze endlessly, or fill the time with activities. You can concentrate on amusing yourself, or on how to be useful. You can take an interest in political affairs, or religious matters, or community service, or sports, or whatever. The choice is yours.

Are you happy to have all your time to yourself (if, indeed, you do), or do you have a more negative response? Do you hate growing older, or feel useless? Do you worry—about money, or your health, or where to live? Are you out of sorts because "There's nothing to do?" You'll find that retirement life reflects a mixture of emotions, many of which are new to you. You have to sort through these, and resolve them in a way which allows you to live in contentment.

In the following pages I suggest ways you can start. First, I discuss putdowns and what to do about them. Then, how to deal with being home so much. As I've already implied, this is not an unmixed blessing. Indeed, it can become a source of unhappiness if you don't face it squarely. You don't want to find yourself drifting through life in a bathrobe.

It's awfully easy to start feeling sorry for yourself. Maybe this won't be true of you. But it is for many. There are things that might make you feel this way. I've already suggested a few—aging, health, money. You may resent ways you're treated, or the many decisions you have to make. You miss your job, you can't find anyone to do things with, there isn't that much to do, anyway etc., etc., etc.

This mix of emotions comes at a time when you face the decisions I discuss later. They can make it difficult to think clearly, if your feelings get in the way. The first months of retirement bring you the need to make choices while you're also adjusting to a new life. I hope I can help—at least, a little.

Dealing with Putdowns

The most important thing is not to be bothered by them. There's a difference between a word or act intended to put you down, and one that arises unconsciously when you're no longer seen as a full-fledged member of working society.

Any one trying to "put you in your place" should be handled the same way you would have done at any other time of life. The response depends on your feelings for the other person, your tolerance of rude behavior, your sense of what's appropriate in the social setting you're in, your willingness to be confrontational, or any number of other factors.

If you're told, "We don't do that any more," you can ask about current practices, or about how the former approach was bettered, or you can say something complimentary about what's being done now. The whole purpose is not to be defensive or argumentative, but admiring of current practices and persons. You can even ask for help in upgrading your understanding.

If you're ignored in a meeting, or your comments dismissed, you can of course stop going to meetings. If you want to persist, you can ask the presiding officer, or a member with whom you have a good relationship, if there's some way you can contribute.

If some one officiously tries to show you how to do something, be thankful, and later do as you choose. If you do accept the help, you can add further thanks later. Otherwise, just let it be.

If someone grabs your arm to 'help' you without asking, gently disengage yourself, and explain how important it is for you to do as much as possible for yourself for as long as possible.

If people assume, incorrectly. that you're no longer able to do certain things, ask them to watch you, see how you do, and ask them to help you improve. Again, say how important it is for you to do as much as you can for as long as you can.

At Home So Much

Being at home during the working week is a shock—there's the temptation to laze, and even spend the day in a bathrobe.

Since you're spending more time at home than previously, there will be a need to re-assess your household responsibilities, and presumably to take on more of them than before.

It's important that you and your housemate re-think how you divide the chores between you. If neither of you is working, the breakdown should be approximately fifty-fifty. If you're the only one retired, you should be carrying more than half the load.

It's also important to get dressed in the morning—it becomes demoralizing to spend the day in pajamas.

More important still is to have a plan for the day, even if it's only a plan to do nothing. In this way, you can feel in control, and you're not just letting life happen to you.

Your planning can be most informal, but it should be intentional, and done regularly. It's truly demoralizing to feel that life is aimless.

A good idea is to get out of the house every day. I've found that spending too much time indoors, especially if alone, is debilitating, even when I've been doing constructive work.

And you should be doing something constructive, besides household chores and resting. It can be physical or mental—it can even be watching TV, as long as this is what you planned, and is not just surfing channels, looking for something to watch.

In brief, your time at home should be spent just as systematically as your time at the office used to be. The only difference is that now you can plan to do exactly what you want to do. The key concept, though, is that you need to do planning.

Feeling Sorry for Yourself

It's easy to fall into a situation where there's no one to do anything with, there's nothing you want to do anyway, you don't feel like doing chores or exercising—in short, you're at loose ends, and without prospects.

In such a situation, it's also easy to feel your life is out of control and without much purpose. From there, it's only a short trip to feeling sorry for yourself.

This feeling can be a by-product of a non-planned period when you have not taken charge, and nothing seems to be happening, or worth doing.

Avoiding this is the best argument for planning. Whether it's for one day (or week or month or year or life), there's no substitute for it, if you want to feel positive about your life.

Another way to avoid feeling sorry for yourself is activity. Almost any kind of activity will do, so long as it is <u>active</u>—napping won't do, nor will watching TV. Nor will reading, if you use it to escape thinking about what you should be doing.

However, walking, exercising, doing chores, running errands, visiting with somebody, or doing almost anything constructive, either with or for someone else, will serve to break the mold.

Still another thing you can try is to direct your thoughts toward people who are close to you, and think about what their needs are. By doing this, you stop dwelling on your own concerns, and your outlook brightens.

The very best thing to do is something that helps someone else. In another part of this book there are suggested things to do which are of value to other people. This type of activity is probably the best way for you to feel positive about yourself.

Adjusting to the New Reality

This is not easy, since many changes come as a surprise. Perhaps I should say, "Catch you unready," since none of them is truly unfamiliar, and all have been observed by you, among friends and family members living in retirement.

But just as the overawing grandeur of the Grand Canyon blows away visitors who <u>thought</u> they already knew what they were going to see, the everyday realities of retirement life seem different when you're experiencing them yourself rather than just observing them.

The preceding two pages paid particular attention to (1) being at home a lot, and (2) having to fight off self-pity. But there are many other adjustment issues, many of which are considered in Chapter 3.

Your principal task is looking at yourself, and asking, "Who do I want to be for the rest of my life? What will make me truly happy? What will make me feel good about myself?" Is there something I really want to accomplish?

Somewhat later in this book I discuss self-understanding, and it is on this that I'm focusing at this time. If you're not used to being introspective, you might like to read Chapter 13.

In short, I'm saying that the large array of changes which take place shortly after retirement can overwhelm you, and cause you to make choices and do things (or not do things) hastily and without reflection—actions you might regret later.

The areas about which you need to think carefully are those I've chosen to discuss in this book. These areas require not only attention to their details, and the suggestions I make, but they ask you to think long and hard about your own nature—what you can handle, what's important to you, what responsibilities you have to others, and what you truly care about.

Chapter 3

Your New Life

Settling In

I've talked about your new image. I've talked about your new you. Now I'll talk about what these add up to—a critical period in your life when you make many changes in a short period of time.

Since retirement is not retiring <u>from</u> something so much as it is retiring <u>to</u> something. I suggest that you acknowledge this reality, and manage your retirement instead of letting it manage you. The plans you make early on should be good for the long run. I've already hinted at this, and the challenges you'll face early on.

In this chapter I consider the decisions you'll have to make and the routines you'll have to establish. In addition, the three most important areas—which deal with your health, where you'll live, and how you'll pay for it all—need more space, and are the subject of the next three chapters. All these issues will arise.

But you'll also have to think about lots of other things—what car you'll drive, whether or not you'll need two, what changes you'll make in your wardrobe, whether to eat out as much as you're used to, how your recreation and entertainment will be different, who you'll be spending time with, what continuing contacts you'll have with the fellow-workers you're leaving behind, and a host of others.

So far as your car is concerned, you'll almost certainly be driving less, and probably doing a different kind of driving. You'll have to consider the age and condition of the car or cars you're now using, and if you'll need a replacement soon. You may find that your new patterns of use make you want a different type of automobile. If you're married, you may also want to think about whether or not the two of you can coordinate around one vehicle.

Changes in your habits will impact your clothing, your scheduling, and your budget. For example, your wardrobe, which formerly had a heavy component of clothes for work, will look different—probably more informal. Consider, too, whether you'll be going out as much (or possibly, more)—for eating, recreation, or entertainment. Perhaps, changes in your income may cause finances to be an issue.

There's the thought of whom you'll be spending time with. Of course, your friends and family remain a constant, although their schedules may no longer match yours as closely as before. But you'll probably be seeing less of your former work-mates. Generally speaking, retired people find their companions more and more from among persons in the same circumstances their own.

Every one's needs will be different, of course, but the areas I've noted will probably come up for most of you. There will be others, too, which I have not have mentioned, or possibly not even have thought of, as I try to visualize everyone's circumstances.

There's no way I can visualize all of you. But I can alert you to the need to be prepared, and not be caught by surprise. It's noteworthy that many people enter retirement without any plan in mind, other than a general feeling that life will be easier. In consequence, they often find themselves unready for it.

In the next two pages I make some suggestions about the decisions you'll make and the routines you should establish. I hope they make you less unready.

Decisions, Decisions, Decisions

You should sit down early in retirement, preferably with anyone you're living with, to consider just what you'll be doing and how you'll be living in the years to come. This can provide a basis for making decisions.

Perhaps the most urgent decision for you to make is about health care, since you're probably on Medicare for the first time.

Next comes where you're going to live, since your needs have changed. You have many choices.

The third major decision has to do with finances; it's third only because most people have already done pre-planning. If you haven't, then it clearly becomes number one. These three are considered in greater detail later.

You have to re-think your wardrobe, since your lifestyle will change.

You have to re-plan your household responsibilities, since you'll be home so much more.

You have to decide what kind and how many cars you'll need.

You need to think about such things as eating out, entertaining and entertainment, and recreational activities. Your opportunities will be different, and so will many of your habits.

Also different will be the friends you'll see regularly—many of course will continue from the past, but many will not.

You need to decide what kind of constructive activities you want to give time and energy to.

In short, you need to see retirement as the start of a whole new life, and you have to make plans for it—not just let it happen haphazardly.

Organizing Routines

Much of the above is about planning. If this is done regularly and systematically, it's the start of creating routines.

Throughout your active years, your job alone did much to organize your day. With working hours, commuting, and lunch breaks, over half your time awake was committed.

Earlier lists present your new challenge—you're home (maybe alone), you're striving to have good feelings, and you're trying to use your time constructively.

In addition to the suggestions I've already made, I'd like to propose some ways to establish routines.

There are have several areas which benefit from this: 1) household responsibilities, 2) community and other forms of service, 3) getting together with family and friends, 4) leisure-time activities, and 5) taking a part- or full-time job.

If you decide to work full-time, of course, your day will be much like it was previously. In effect, you're not retired—yet.

I suggest that you decide, from among the above areas, those you intend to give time to (there are many suggestions in Part 2 of this book).

Use a daytimer or something similar, in which you schedule times and details for the activities you choose. This should be as precise and detailed as it was when you worked.

Although later in this book I urge you to be flexible, I think that, at least at the beginning of retirement, you should have as regular a schedule for each activity you as you did for your responsibilities when you had a job. For instance, you can decide to go to the library every Monday, Wednesday, or Friday; or plan to walk every morning at 8 a.m., if the weather's good, or whatever—but make it a regular practice.

CHAPTER 4

How Do I Stay Healthy?

The 900lb. Gorilla

You've all heard the joke, "Where does a 900-lb. gorilla sleep?" The answer: "Wherever he wants to." Medicare is going to be the 900-lb. gorilla in your life.

It's not the only health issue you'll have to deal with, but it's such a dominant factor that I start this chapter with it.

One of the first things you deal with in retirement, then, is Medicare. And it's not going to go away, since you'll be on it for the rest of your life. All existing health coverage changes at age 65, and all plans assume your primary insurer will become Medicare. (I suppose it's possible that my use of the word, 'all,' is a little over-blown, since it's conceivable that a few people in unique or unusual situations might have something different. Still, what I have to say applies to everybody I know or have heard of.)

Even those of you who've been continuously protected by a plan offered through your employer will now find your primary coverage is Medicare. You may have been part of a group plan before, but you're in a different group now, where decisions revolve around the program's payment practices.

Medicare is both a boon and a bane. It's a boon because everybody is eligible for it. It's a bane because everyone has to deal with its cumbersome procedures and requirements. Like all huge bureaucracies, it's difficult to find real persons to talk to, to get answers to questions, and to process complaints. But it's important for you to inform yourself fully about the system. The remarks I make below can give you some inkling of its approach. But I don't pretend to be an expert, and suggest that you get help from qualified persons.

Medicare determines what amount it will approve as payment for any health service provided. Then, it actually pays 80% of that amount to the server, expecting the patient to pay the rest. (It also has an annual deductible for the patient to pay.) Many people arrange to purchase backup insurance (called Medigap insurance) to cover what they'd otherwise have to pay. However, there are signs that in the future the annual deductible, and perhaps other amounts, may not be totally covered by it. If you have backup insurance (which of course you pay for) you usually will not have to lay out any money for services you receive.

Most physicians and medical organizations now accept the amounts approved by Medicare as full payment for their services, although when the program first came into existence, it didn't work this way. At that time, professional servers charged their usual rates to patients, received a Medicare payment, and expected the patients to cover the balance. But this resulted in so much confusion and unhappiness on the part of patients, and so much difficulty and expense in the server's office that the profession gradually came to the state it's in today. Now, medical professionals receive Medicare's portion of the approved amount, and the unpaid percentage from the patient or the backup insurer.

Some people close the payment gap by signing with an HMO (Health Maintenance Organization, as if you didn't know), which undertakes to cover all costs, except a modest co-pay for each service. People who've signed up with an HMO find the organization basically accepts Medicare payments as full coverage for the services they provide. The patient has only to make the co-payment. However, if you go this way, you have the limitation that you can use only the professionals provided or approved by the HMO.

So far as hospitals are concerned, Medicare pays 100% of everything it approves, after an initial annual deductible. But it doesn't pay for service in nursing facilities, retirement residences, or assisted living, other than short periods associated with a hospital stay. If these expenses are a concern to you, you should look into specialized insurance, or make the costs part of your overall financial planning, or both.

One problem in all this is the way Medicare calculates the amounts it approves. It uses what it calls the "average payment" for any given service, as charged by local professionals. However, the organization uses figures from prior years, when fees were lower. Further, the figures come from a wide geographic area, with all levels of economic conditions, and of course variance in age, experience, and competence among the professionals. (Remember—as many as half of all doctors In America may have graduated in the bottom 50 percent of their class.)

So, your doctor or other health professional will probably receive from Medicare considerably less than was paid on your behalf before you retired, and considerably less than she considers her services to be worth. This will usually represent no change in the treatment and personnel you're accustomed to. But it can cause you inconvenience if you move to a different locale, or have to join a new practice. Many servers are reluctant to take on new Medicare patients. If their services are in demand, they can improve their income by saving places for those who, individually or through insurance, can pay a higher rate.

Remember, then, that any servers who accept Medicare as their basis of payment, are, in effect, giving you a major senior-citizen discount. And even if you wish to add something extra by way of appreciation, you can't do so. A health professional with Medicare patients is not permitted to serve them at all if she accepts additional payment from any one of them.

If you can, you should try to avoid changing health professionals after going on Medicare. If you have to do so, see if you can enlist the help of the physician whose practice you're leaving, to see if she can help you secure a place with some one new.

Sooner or later, though, especially as you get older, you'll need specialists, or other health personnel, for new conditions that arise, and you'll have the challenge of locating new helpers. You need to start thinking now about getting recommendations and references you can rely on. If you have a family physician whom you like and trust, she can be a great help. Of course, if you're a member of an HMO this problem will not arise, although it's still quite possible you'll be dealing with new people.

You need to learn how Medicare functions, and the options you have. This includes finding out about Medicare Part D (its plan for helping with prescription medicines)—one of the most complicated programs I've ever seen. There's no way I could cover all this in a brief space, even assuming that I knew enough to do so.

Medicare's Plan D is actually a number of different programs, since it allows various drug suppliers and other organizations to offer plans under their approval. In these, customers can obtain prescriptions at sharply discounted rates, until the total retail value of their purchases in any given year reaches a certain amount ($2830.00 in 2010). This is not the amount the customers actually paid, but the full retail cost of the medicines they've purchased.

Once this level is reached, the buyers pay full price, until the total value reaches another fixed amount ($4550.00 in 2010). Thereafter, costs are considered to be catastrophic, and Medicare pays all or almost all of anything further. The in-between period, when you pay everything, is widely known as the 'doughnut hole,' and resulted from compromises in Congress at the time the original legislation was enacted.

I've given the figures for 2010 above, but they change every year, and both will be higher, although probably not sharply, in the future. Also, there is now the intention to eliminate the doughnut hole eventually. In the meantime, the government will provide amounts (currently, a maximum of $250.00—but due to increase yearly) of financial assistance toward making the payments called for by it.

As for prescriptions from HMO's, each has its own procedures. But I believe they all have an arrangement whereby members are able to obtain medications at sharply reduced prices. Since my own coverage is Medicare plus Medigap, I'm more familiar with that approach than with HMO's. Also, since procedures vary from one HMO to another, it's difficult to make generalizations.

Another aspect of Medicare I'd like to discuss is its position regarding alternative medicine and medications. For example, acupuncture is not covered by it, although there are rumors that it may be at some future time. (I hear that time has already come.)

Alternative medications are also not covered, basically because they're over-the-counter items. I think it's safe to say that Medicare will not pay for anything alternative. However, if you think you have a special situation, you should check to see if there is anything available. Physical therapy is covered, although of course it has to be prescribed by a physician.

I haven't considered long-term-care insurance. As most of you probably know already, this is a way to get help with at least part of the cost of nursing care. It's not easy to give a quick overview of this subject, since many variables are involved. If you're interested, you should look into several plans before you decide on any. I can say, though, that the younger you are when you buy this insurance, the lower the premium will be, although of course, you'll probably pay for it for a longer time before you have to call upon it.

Other variables include the monthly amount the policy will pay toward nursing care, the lifetime total of such payments, whether or not there is a limited time for the payments to be made, whether or not the amounts are adjusted for inflation, and if the policy covers care at home. The whole area is complex, difficult to understand, and requires as much help as you can manage. For some people it's exceedingly desirable; for others, it's not.

And now, I must give a warning. Although I've tried to be careful in describing constraints and conditions, there's always the possibility of error. You should take my remarks as giving a reasonably accurate sketch of the whole picture, while you take pains to get authoritative answers to all questions of concern to you. Your approach to how your health costs will be covered in the future will have to serve you the rest of your life, so you must be sure it is both reliable, and something you can live with.

There are more aspects to your health needs, though, than how they're paid for. Maybe this isn't the best place to discuss those aspects of your behavior which contribute (or don't contribute) to your health throughout a long life. A number of these are considered in later parts of this book. Still, I feel I should include couple of thoughts while still on the subject of your earliest days of retirement.

The first is something I've learned to do, and which my doctor believes to be important if I want to stay in the best possible health. That is, get into the habit of knowing my own body.

This is not to say that I recommend your doing self-diagnosis, or deciding what medications you need, or bringing to your doctor's attention the latest findings you read in a newspaper or magazine, or hear on TV. Instead, it amounts to taking the time to look at what happens in your life, and what changes occur in your body. My doctor says no one knows your body better than you do, and the more objectively you observe and report changes that have taken place, together with the circumstances in which they occurred, the better able a health professional is to treat you.

One way to do this is to start a health journal. In it, you can record any noticeable changes which have occurred—incidents of dizziness or loss of balance, unusual aches or pains, moments of weakness, digestive or intestinal difficulties, or anything else of an unusual nature. You should describe what happened as objectively as possible, without including your opinion about the cause. State what you were doing, and what were the circumstances at the time of the incident, specifically including the period of time preceding it.

However, whether you keep a journal or not, you should, when you visit a health professional, report bodily changes and circumstances as descriptively as possible. If the helper cuts you short, or doesn't appear interested, I suggest you look for another server. It's not too much to say that early recognition and treatment of health needs are essential for a long life, and your willingness to observe and report observations is the first line of defense. Some people find certain things embarrassing, especially those dealing with intestinal matters or their sex life. You may have to acquire an extra measure of will-power to make sure that these areas are not overlooked.

My second point is to note that once you stop work, your life patterns change remarkably! You're less active, you rush less, you don't have to grab and gulp food. In short, you've become a person of leisure. This means, if you're not careful, that you may also become a sedentary person—a couch potato.

A leisurely lifestyle can be good, as well as bad. It's good if you use the luxury of eating in a relaxed way to avoid fast-food, high-calorie, high-transfat items. It's good if you replace hours of rushing around with a calmer, more comfortable way of life. It's bad, though, if you don't change any old bad practices—if, once you're fully in control of your life, you don't develop the habits of good health and positive behavior which will lead you to 100—items that I spend much of the balance of this volume discussing.

I know this sounds pollyannish. It echoes the preachments you've received all your life—from earliest childhood. I'll try to avoid platitudes and limit myself to what I've actually learned from experience—from what I did, or didn't do, as I struggled on my path to old age. I'll also try to give you the thinking behind my remarks. If any of it is of help to you, I'll feel my efforts have been worth doing.

Medicare

You have to learn about Medicare, since almost every retired person gets her health coverage that way, unless she has insurance through a job at which she (or her spouse) is still working

Medicare distributes a big, big, BIG book every year, called <u>Medicare and You</u>, The 2010 edition has 128 pages. Get it and read it, and, if necessary, call to get help understanding it.

Remember, though, that Medicare is a huge bureaucracy, and be prepared for difficulties in getting answers, having complaints heard, or even getting a live voice on the telephone.

Recognize that Medicare pays health providers at a lower rate than they receive from other patients. You may find it hard to obtain services from a new provider. If you do have to change physicians, or be referred to a specialist, see if you can get the professionals currently serving you to help.

Look into insurance that's a backup to Medicare, as well as HMO's which accept Medicare as full payment.

There's a wide variety of organizations providing Medigap insurance. AARP is one. Often, your retirement association is another.

Kaiser Permanente is perhaps the best known of the HMO's, and it has a good reputation. However, there are many others with a good reputation, too. If you look into one, try to speak with one or more persons who use it, to find how satisfied they are.

If you use Medicare to cover a hospital stay, be sure to get a detailed statement, and review it carefully. Hospitals have been known to make mistakes and bill for items the patient did not receive. Also, they're notorious for charging outrageously. You should question anything you don't feel right about. Remember, if Medicare consistently overpays, it could eventually affect the stability of everyone's coverage.

Making Health Decisions

Your costs for health care will almost certainly be greater than you anticipate, especially when you consider prescription drugs and matters not covered by Medicare, e.g., nursing care, acupuncture, health clubs, and over-the-counter items.

Also, these expenses will increase steadily, due to the workings of inflation, and your ever-growing health needs.

Inform yourself about costs for long-term care (assisted living and/or nursing facilities), and consider how you will deal with them. If necessary, look into insurance for this purpose.

A great many older people run out of money (except, possibly, for Social Security), and must rely on Medicaid for long-term nursing care. However, before this is available to you, you have to spend down virtually all your assets.

Even items held in joint tenancy with another person are subject to this requirement in many places. Only the half, or other percentage, owned by the other joint tenant is exempt.

In many states, if one of a married couple goes into a nursing facility, she will not be eligible for Medicaid payments until her spouse's assets are also fairly well drained. You can't get around this requirement by putting funds in someone else's name. Such an action can be reversed if the need for Medicaid arises before five years have elapsed.

Look into various programs which provide assistance in paying for medications. Of course, Medicare - Part D helps here, but there are other sources of help. (Medicare - Part D is such an important factor that I deal with it extensively in another list.)

Let your doctor know if you have financial problems in dealing with your health needs. She may know of resources that can help. Also, rely on the counsel of knowledgeable senior advisors.

Getting Prescription Medicines

Medicare - Part D is the place to start. Although when I first attended an orientation session I was so overwhelmed by the amount of information—seemingly conflicting information— that I almost gave up.

A large number of plans are offered by insurance and other companies, as well as various organizations, all of them accepted by Medicare. These plans vary in the amount they pay and the medications they cover. They also vary from state to state. (I just checked my state (Colorado) and found 48 plans.)

Knowing where to start is a challenge. If you can find a good advisor, go there. If you're a member of a retirement organization, ask if they can help (they may have their own plan). Or, you can get help from AARP, which also has a plan.

I hate to recommend using a computer because there are so many senior citizens without them, or without the knowhow to try. Still, click "Medicare - Part D" on Google, or ask someone to do it for you, and see now much information you get.

You're often advised to find the plan which offers the best deal for the most expensive medicine you take regularly. On the website I mentioned, you can search to see how, in your own state, different plans charge for any drug you specify.

You might note that there are some time constraints for applying for a plan. When you're first eligible for Medicare, you have a 7-month period, surrounding your 65th birthday, within which you can apply. Every year thereafter, there's a time frame when you can change. If you go outside it, there's a penalty.

You can apply to the manufacturer of an expensive medication you take regularly, to see if they can offer any help. Often, they can.

In view of all the above, I can't help but feel you're going to have to ask some knowledgeable person for assistance.

Dealing with Doctors

It is absolutely essential that you both like and trust your doctor. So do not stay with one about whom you have reservations. Do not talk yourself into continuing with such a one, saying, "I don't know anyone else," or "I'm used to her now," or "She has such a good reputation."

If you do stay with a doctor you have doubts about, you'll find you often don't tell her all you should, you doubt some of the things she tells you to do, and, in general, you don't have the feeling of confidence and optimism you need if your medical treatment is going to do its best for you.

You should follow your doctor's suggestions precisely, or if not, make an explanation on your next visit. Take all your medications in exactly the manner and amount prescribed.

You should be your own heath observer, noting and describing symptoms as they arise, and what preceded and followed each. Don't hesitate to include everything. Let the doctor tell you if you're going into too much detail, or including matters too minor to mention.

You should keep a record of symptoms, and the conditions when they appeared. Write down questions, or concerns, and take them when you go see the doctor. You want to make sure all your needs are considered.

If the doctor appears disinterested, GET A NEW DOCTOR.

My doctor reminds me that no one knows the patient's body as well as the patient himself, and he asks me to do the kind of observation and reporting I've just described.

A positive approach to your health is the best way to assure its continuance. You cannot be positive unless you and your doctor are a team. Again I say, "DO NOT STAY WITH A PHYSICIAN YOU DO NOT LIKE AND TRUST!

Preventive Medicine

You've all heard about preventive medicine from the time your mother said, "Eat your vegetables—they're good for you."

I'm going to repeat certain things you've been told, because they're more important now than they ever were.

I'll not comment on such things as the benefits of whole grains, the dangers of transfats and red meat, and how many portions of vegetables and fruit you should consume daily. This information is too detailed to be included, it's available widely, and I probably would not be complete and accurate enough.

Instead, I'll talk about why we don't pay more attention to it. It's boring, it requires a lot of time and effort, it may cost more, and for many people the resulting food is not as tasty as the sinful alternatives—like Big Macs and fries.

Remember that you now have the time to be careful, and your aging body doesn't handle misuse as well as it did. You no longer have to eat on the run. So take time to learn about foods that are both healthy and delicious. Pay attention and take care!

However, preventive medicine is more than eating right. It also includes healthy habits like exercise, getting enough sleep, seeing your dentist and following his advice, having regular checkups, and cultivating a relaxed lifestyle. The secret to longevity is to know what helps and hinders, and make a plan to live healthy. This book is designed to help you do this.

Unfortunately, medical insurance often does not reward preventive steps, even though such action may well cost less than the illnesses which might otherwise be avoided. Don't follow their practice just to save money. Any resulting illnesses might cost you less if you're properly insured, but they'll cost you more in pain and suffering, and may shorten your life.

Prevention is the best health insurance you will ever have.

Obesity

Perhaps I'm taking on a responsibility which should be assigned to a doctor or dietitian. But I have something to say.

First, everyone knows obesity is unhealthy, can shorten your life, can predispose you to various illnesses, and is often very difficult to reverse, or even prevent. So you've already heard it all.

Further, if you've had a lifelong weight problem, it becomes even harder to control as a retiree, with lots of time and leisure (and possibly a need for comfort) to overeat.

I'm not going to tell you to diet, cut back on your favorite foods, or count your calories. Instead, I'm going to make only one suggestion.

Keep a food diary! Make a resolution to write down everything you put in your mouth—meals, snacks, odd-bites, whatever. You don't need to use any numbers, such as the time, the amount eaten, or fat grams, or calories.

Of course, if you want to enter some figures in your food diary, like calories or fat grams, there's no reason not to. Still, the diary alone is an important tool.

You'll find this method will cause you to be more conscious of how much and how often you eat. This very fact alone may cause you to slow down. For example, you may find that a single bite of something is too much trouble to enter in the diary. A reduction in the number of single bites is a help.

You may also find that if keeping a record helps lower your intake, the amount of weight improvement you obtain is both modest and continuous. This is the kind of weight loss which can become permanent, because it leads to a change in your eating habits.

Smoking

How does one say something about smoking which is both original and helpful? The answer is that one doesn't. Yet the topic has to be included because of its health implications.

Everyone knows that smokers have a shorter life span than others on average, and that they're prone to more diseases.

At the same time, the habit is a great comfort to many people—even those who wish they could quit.

I'm not going to counsel anyone to quit because this is such a personal decision, and most smokers have debated the pro's and con's many times. If you're a smoker, it's up to you.

Smoking in retirement has to be considered anew like so much else. You may get into close contact with others, especially in later life, so the issue of secondhand smoke has to be a concern. Also, older retirees may find it difficult or even impossible to go outdoors to smoke.

You need an arrangement, if you haven't already got one, to ensure your smoke does not impact anyone with whom you share quarters, including the smell of tobacco.

In your own home, it's usually possible to devise a place which is well-ventilated, and separate from the general living quarters.

In a retirement residence or nursing home, the situation is more difficult. All of them have rules, and the smoker must know if she can abide by them before she ever enters. It may be possible to smoke in your own space, or in some specially-designated location.

Perhaps, the smoker-retiree might want to re-think her habit when she re-thinks the rest of her lifestyle. There's no doubt that avoiding the use of tobacco will improve her chance to be 100.

CHAPTER 5

Where Do I Live?

Home, Sweet Roam

"What do you mean—Where do I live? I've already got a place to live!"

True! True! But will you be able to afford it after you retire? Will you need that much space? Have you been looking forward to moving to a warmer climate, or closer to your children?

For some people, the choice of where to live is urgent once they retire. You may be one of them. Probably, though, you can defer the decision. Many people stay for a long time in the same home they've been in. However, sooner of later, you'll have to make some choices about housing.

Your lifestyle has changed. You doubtless have no children at home, and probably no other dependents, as well. The large house seems empty. It demands a lot of time and care. Your needs are different, and perhaps your finances. In this chapter I discuss come of the possibilities you may want to consider.

An early question often is, "Do I want to live someplace else?" Your children may not be nearby, you may wish a community with a lower cost of living, or a more relaxed lifestyle—perhaps without snow. You might like to be closer to shopping and services.

You should know that moving to another community can be very traumatic. It may be that some persons making such a move shortly after retirement have an increased rate of accidents and illness—and a shorter life span.

If you do consider doing this, remember that it works best if you've had extensive contact with the new community before you go there to live. If you've spent time in a vacation home in the area, of course you already know what you're getting into, and with lots of contacts and information, you don't need any advice from me.

But, if you haven't had extensive prior experience there, you should think about making one or more lengthy visits to the location, renting instead of buying, to see how well you adjust, and if its appeal lasts. A move to another area is arduous, time-consuming, and expensive. You want to be sure you're not going to regret it.

Transferring to a new location is the most challenging of your housing options. But there are many others. You can plan to stay in your own home, you can move into an apartment, or you can sell the house and buy something smaller—for example, .a condominium or mobile home Incidentally, if you're thinking of an apartment, you should know there are places specifically designed for seniors, with a number of special amenities. I discuss them later.

In all the above, I've been making the assumption that you presently live in a house you own. If this isn't the case for you, your decisions may be easier. But the alternatives are much the same—stay where you are, move elsewhere, get something smaller, rent or buy.

If you're living alone, you may be thinking about joint accommodations with a friend or relative. In a later section of this book, I discuss the question of sharing quarters (Chapter 25). You might look at it. Or perhaps you've been invited to live with a child or other family member. Still, many of the same considerations apply. This, too, is considered later.

One type of housing I haven't mentioned is the retirement residence. I discuss this in its own chapter in Part 3. But I don't deal with it at this time, since it rarely applies to the newly retired. Part 3 deals with the issues of later retirement days.

A housing decision is not easy to make, since everything has its advantages and disadvantages. In the lists following this chapter. I try to give the pro's and con's of various choices. I've kept each list short, and obviously don't fully cover the ground for anything you might seriously consider. All you'll get are a few pointers, indicating things you might want to look into.

Many friends or family members may urge you to do this or that. So you have to make your decision under a certain amount of pressure. Be careful! In the end, a great deal depends on your personality and that of others in your family. While no action is urgent, the housing question will nag you until you settle it.

Try to anticipate the needs, problems, and difficulties which could arise, and then sort out the various suggestions and pieces of advice you are offered.

Remember—it's the rest of your life you're planning for.

Moving to a New Location

<u>Pro's</u>

You may well be closer to family and/or friends.

You can select a place with a lifestyle and/or a climate that suit you.

You may be able to locate where costs are lower.

You can go to a place that attracts you with recreation, shopping, college or university, museums, theater, medical facilities, etc.

You can live in the size of community, with the amount of urbanization, that you want.

<u>Con's</u>

There's a lot of work, stress, and expense in making a move.

You leave friends, familiar surroundings, and those who serve you.

Setting up in a new area is stressful, with the challenge of learning how to get around, finding new sources of help and service, and establishing new habit patterns.

New residents in an area may be subject to more accidents, breakdowns, and illnesses than they've been before.

If you regret the move, additional pressure is put on you, whether to stay on, or consider moving back—or elsewhere. If you do move again, you'll be subject to a lot of expense.

Take a lot of time making such a big decision, which is a total re-make of your lifestyle. The risk of being wrong by staying where you are is much less than that of being wrong by moving.

Staying in Your Home

Pro's

No muss, no fuss, no expense, no strain.

No one is put to the task of helping.

You already know what the obligations and benefits are.

You don't have to notify anybody of a new address and circumstance.

You're totally familiar with the amenities and services available in the area.

You don't have to find new people or places to be of service to you.

Con's

You may not want the responsibilities of being a householder any longer.

It may be too hard to keep up.

The house may well be aging, and need major work in the future (e.g., painting, roof replacement, gutters, windows, cement).

The expenses of the house may be more than you want to carry.

You may have a lot of equity tied up that you'd like to access.

The house may be too big for comfort.

Apartment Living

<u>Pro's</u>

It's usually cheaper.

It may well be closer to transportation and shopping.

Neighbors may be able to watch and give help.

When something goes wrong, it's the landlord's or manager's job to fix it.

You can leave, if necessary, on short notice.

It's usually easier to control the temperature indoors.

<u>Con's</u>

Landlord may be slow to address problems.

You live in close quarters, with neighbors who may be noisy.

A difficult or unfriendly neighbor can be a problem.

It can be difficult, impossible, and/or expensive to fix up the place as you would like.

Storage may be a problem.

Apartment living may feel confining, if you've been in a house.

You may not want to give up gardening.

You're usually tied to a lease, so moving on short notice may be costly.

Condominiums

Pro's

You're still building equity, and getting tax deductions.

Like apartments, condos can be close to transportation and shopping.

You have many of the advantages of a house, without outdoor responsibilities.

You usually have more space than an apartment, but less than most houses.

You can usually find more variety of size and internal arrangements than in an apartment.

You have a sense of community with your neighbors.

You can have a voice in important decisions, through participation in the homeowners' association.

Con's

You also have all the disadvantages of control by a homeowners' association, whose decisions you may not always like.

You may not be able to make the exterior changes you wish.

You're vulnerable to rate increases or assessments.

You've tied up a chunk of your capital, and/or burdened yourself with big payments.

Noise and neighbors can present the same problems as in an apartment.

Storage can be a problem.

Mobile Homes

Many people try to save money on their housing by living in an inexpensive mobile home in a trailer park. Their dwelling is on wheels, was delivered complete from the factory, and mounted on a permanent or semi-permanent foundation.

Such a place is purchased, or rented, either new or after a previous use, just like a regular house.

This choice is often made by those without much cash or credit resources. Frequently, such people don't have even a down payment for a mobile home, and find that renting one is a low-price approach to housing.

The savings in trailer living come at the cost of several disadvantages. These include cramped quarters, crowded neighborhoods—often in a poor part of town—and, frequently, lack of the protection of a lease.

Some people purchase a mobile home in which to live. This insures their accommodations are a good fit for their needs, and their expenditures are within their means.

But there are also problems with this approach—among them are again the tight quarters. There may be difficulty in locating space in an acceptable trailer court, and problems getting a loan to finance the purchase. There is also the uncomfortable realization that one owns a property which depreciates and declines in value.

Another disadvantage is that the owner does not own the land under his home, and the rent for the site can always be raised, or the trailer court sold, and the site become unavailable. He might have to move expensively. Also, the municipality might require unexpected and/or costly changes.

For many, a mobile home is a benefit—for others, not. If interested, try it first on a rental basis, before making a big outlay of money.

Recreational Vehicles

Some retirees, especially those with ample funds, use a trailer, or an RV, as a way to move around the country. You might think of them as endless vacationers, avid sightseers, climate chasers, or devoted family members. This option was not discussed in the text of the chapter, since it applies to very few.

What these people are doing is setting up a new residence in which to dwell, either full-time, or a great deal of the time. Everything I've said about moving to a new locality applies to them.

For those whose wish is to do this, there's the pleasure of spending time in places with desirable scenery, climate, or facilities, and of visiting distant friends and family members.

The disadvantages again include owning a depreciating property. There's also the difficulty of maintaining a relationship with health servers, and possible problems if a medical emergency arises in a strange location

Cost may be a major consideration, since in addition to a depreciating asset, there's expense for gasoline, for vehicle maintenance and repair, for space in trailer parks, and for the usual outlays involved in travel and sightseeing.

There's difficulty in maintaining your contacts in the community where you formerly resided. This can become more of a problem as you age, and find the tasks of extensive highway driving and vehicle maintenance burdensome.

In short, life in an RV may be a pleasant experience. But it is not a permanent solution for retirement living—though it may be satisfactory for a long time.

For many, this kind of life is a joy—for others, not. If interested, you should try it first on a rental basis, before making a big outlay of money.

CHAPTER 6

How Do I Pay for It?

Money Matters!

Paying for it is the everlasting challenge we all face again and again. I'm not sure how helpful I can be to anyone who has repeatedly had to make financial decisions.

I make the assumption, not only that you've been doing this for years, but that you've already been thinking about how to handle such matters after retirement. You've doubtless received lots of advice and acquired much information on the subject. Still, it's possible you could be making finances your first concern, and asking the question, "How do I pay for it?"

Finding an answer means knowing how much money you've got, and how much everything will cost. The first is easier to predict than the second. Most of you have had Social Security payments withheld during your working life. Many have a pension or IRA or 401(k), or something similar, or some combination of these—plus (hopefully!) savings and other assets, like equity in a house. So you can estimate your income fairly effectively, relying on known, fixed-dollar amounts from Social Security and pensions, plus recommendations and projections from investment advisors. All this may make you think your financial arrangements are in order. In a way, that's so; in a way, it's not.

Your income is not the whole story. You also need to know your expenses.

And this is not as easy as it looks. For one thing, many people don't budget, but rather allocate money to certain known items, like car loans, house payments, or utility bills, and spend the rest as the need or desire arises. Frequently, there's a shortage at the end of the month, and they close the gap by using credit cards. The end-result may well be that they get into debt almost without knowing it, and perhaps to a sizable extent. They then face the task of getting reorganized.

If this hasn't ever happened to you, you're not only fortunate, but you've shown the ability to manage finances. You've made your own good fortune, and you really don't need anything more that I can say. But for every one else, I'll note that the pattern described above doesn't work very well in retirement.

You can no longer look forward to a raise or a bonus, or a better job, or moonlighting to close a gap between income and outlay. (Although, of course, you can always consider full- or part-time employment.) Mostly, the money you get is all you have, and it's almost certainly not going to change a whole lot for the rest of your life. Furthermore, if you <u>do</u> decide to work after retirement, you're likely to find the pay lower than you were used to.

So, it's important to find out what you face. Your expenses have changed materially by eliminating the cost of going to work. But there may be new ones, especially if you have plans for travel, or leisure-time activity.

I suggest that for the first six months after you retire, you keep a record of what you actually spend, so that you know what your needs will look like. I'm not going to use the word, 'budget,' because I know many of you don't like the thought. However, you <u>can</u> make better decisions if you have good information.

You should find out what you're spending your money for. I'm sure you think you already know. But when I've done this myself, as I have occasionally, I'm always surprised at what sneaked into the picture while I wasn't noticing. There are often many small, casual purchases that fall below the radar, but which truly add up in a month. Or larger outlays, which are rationalized as being one-time only, or not so large as to be a problem, or both. So please take my suggestion seriously.

Once you find out where your money is actually going, you're in a position to decide if that's where you want it to go. Do you really want to eat out that much and spend that much at restaurants? Are the movies (and snack bar) worth it? Or Starbucks? Or other self-indulgences? Are there more important things to use your dollars for? Casual purchases often make a bigger hole in our pockets than we realize. So, looking at your outlay is a major step toward gaining control and security in retirement.

Remember, too, that closing the gap with credit cards is a little more serious now that you're retired. Each month that you do this is a month in which your expenditures are greater than your revenue. And unless you have some unusual opportunity to increase your income, your next month has the double responsibility of staying in balance, while making up the imbalance of the month before.

A few months of out-of-balance finances can put you into debt, with a major reorganization problem. I know all this is simple common sense, and you've heard it all before. Still, you should remember that retirement is not just like 'all before.' Most ways of increasing your income are gone. And your lifelong security hangs in the balance. So, financial stability is more crucial as it ever was.

In the following lists I make a few suggestions. I hope they're helpful.

Making Financial Decisions

Calculate your fixed income from Social Security, pensions, and other sources. Add your estimated return on investments, and/or your draw from capital. In this way, you'll get an idea what revenue you can count on.

Decide on what activities, with their costs, will be part of your new life.

Make a six-month record of your present actual expenditures. <u>Add</u> the estimated cost of new outlays after retirement. <u>Subtract</u> amounts for present items which will be eliminated or reduced. Compare these figures with what actually occurs later.

If you wait until after you retire to do this—keep a six-month record of expenditures, and see if you like your spending habits.

List separately the items which recur every month and those that don't.

Keep these two areas apart, perhaps by having a different bank account for each. It's easier to make decisions when you look at them separately.

The former will be more difficult to adjust than the latter. It's hard to change amounts spent on regular items because many are obligatory. Irregular items are easier to manage because they're often elective.

However, irregular items may have the big surprises in them—non-recurring items which may be quite large—trips, moves, cars, etc. Recording all but the non-recurring ones for a year or more will give you a sound basis for estimating future outlays.

Continue to watch expenditures carefully, noting any material differences from what was projected. Decide if these reflect decisions which you meant to take.

Making It Last

You should repeat the kind of analysis suggested above whenever there's a major change in your life circumstances, especially in either your income or expenses.

If you find that this analysis shows your assets are not likely to last as long as you do, major measures are needed.

Depending on your age and physical condition, such measures might include taking a job to earn income, doing things for yourself that you've been paying to have done, consulting with a financial advisor to determine if your assets are doing as well as possible, moving to less expensive living quarters, or making serious cuts in your discretionary spending.

What you should <u>not</u> do is use credit cards to close financial gaps, especially for regular expenses. All this does is delay the moment of truth and add finance charges (and possible penalties), to your other burdens. Probably, if you've been doing this, you should destroy the cards.

Today, we're all living longer (a fact of which this book is an acknowledgment). So the projections you or your advisors made, early on, should be re-visited as you get older. It's reasonable for you to plan on needing money until you're 100.

For those in dire need, there are government programs, like SSI and Medicaid, which provide funds to assist them. However, this assistance supports only a poor level of lifestyle, and institutions which accept government money to care for older people are not noted for the quality of their performance.

In brief, you are responsible for yourself. You <u>must not</u> hide your head in the sand, and fail to anticipate the future.

You really don't want to put yourself in the position of asking your family for help, or being forced to live with a family member because you can't afford anything else.

Saving Money

Shop the specials at the grocery store, but don't spend more on gas than you save.

Use some of your extra time to check the newspaper ads, and take advantage of them.

If you eat out, do so at lunchtime, which often offers much the same menu as dinner for a lower price. Remember, too, that many places have early-bird specials in the evening.

Locate the nearest gas station with low prices, and try to buy there exclusively, taking advantage of when you're in its neighborhood.

One of the benefits of retirement living is that you don't need to spend as much on clothing, both because you don't have to dress up so often and because everyday clothes become more casual, and more wash-and-wear. Retirement also makes it easier to buy items at out-of-season sales.

A great many people save money shopping at thrift stores, especially when they have specials. Even if you don't like the idea of second-hand clothing, there are many household items, books, and other usable things at giveaway prices.

Planning joint shopping trips with others can reduce transportation costs, unless too much is spent on lunches and drinks.

There are special services in every community, offering free or low-cost help to seniors on legal matters, income tax returns, job searches, and other problems. Acquaint yourself with them.

Consider doing yourself some of the chores you've hired done in the past—cleaning, yard work, car-washing, etc.

Movies cost less in the daytime.

PART 2
– *The Long Haul* –
The Golden Years?

It's during this stretch that people build the habits and conditions which determine how happy and comfortable they'll be in the time ahead—how long and capably they'll live. It's during this stretch that the practice of positive habits and the avoidance of poor ones will contribute to how gracefully they'll age.

You, too, face the same prospect.

Central to it all is the way you adjust your lifestyle during this time. Listed below are five ways of doing this which I've identified—ways to maximize your prospects for a long life:

1. **Being active**
2. **Looking ahead**
3. **Being independent**
4, **Doing things of value**
5. **Exhibiting empathy**

These five points represent the essence of everything I say in this book. Every suggestion I make can be viewed as a proposal to do something tied to at least one of them. To me, they <u>are</u> the way to live to be 100!

They represent my thoughts on what I think you should <u>do</u>, while the following refers to what you should <u>be</u>:

1. Understanding of self
2. Understanding of others
3. Upbeat
4. Un-rigid

I apologize for the awkwardness of the above. It's occasioned by my wish to create acronyms to help you remember the principal points. (Acronyms are widely used today—and at my advanced age, I must stay current.) They <u>do</u> seem to help, though. Awkward or not, or however I may use (or misuse) the English language, the nine basic ideas above are what I believe, and encourage you to adopt. They are described in Chapter 7, and developed further in later chapters.

CHAPTER 7

A.L.I.V.E. 4U

(at 100?) (For you!)

Many of the things you'll do during the long period I've just described will be what you've been doing all your life. But, later on, you'll have to abridge or amend many of them. I discuss all that in Part 3.

Right now my concern is your vigorous period. This is when the 'Golden Years' set in, if they are to do so at all. It's also the time when your lifestyle will determine not only how golden your years are, but how many of them you'll live to see. I know you've been besieged with endless advice on how to live well and long, I'm sorry to say I'm about to do the same.

I'm going to try to make it as palatable as possible, though, and give my reasons for saying what I do. We often read that certain habits and practices tend to increase your life span, and certain ones do the opposite. So, I recommend you adopt the former and avoid the latter. (Surprise! Surprise!) Many of these suggestions reflect my own life experiences.

Numerous books have been written about longevity. And many centenarians have been interviewed and studied. Though there is no real certainty about how to ensure a long life, there does seem to be a consensus about some things that help. I'm going to discuss these, and I've created an acronym to help you remember.

The acronym is ALIVE!, since that's what I hope you'll be at 100 years of age. It's made up of the initial letters of five practices I hope you'll adopt. These are particularly important during the time when you're still vigorous and active, and feel much as you did during your working years. I fear, though, that you may be tempted to continue the behavior you developed then—not watching your health and your habits because you were so busy.

That approach won't work during retirement. For one thing, bad habits are cumulative, and in time wear down your health and your resistance. For another, bad habits are insidious. Like fatty foods, they feel good and they're seductive, while producing an undesirable end-result.

Retirement at 65—or before or after—might be thought of as the beginning of your old age. (It's certainly widely accepted as the start of senior citizenship.) And it's the time many of our physical attributes— strength, agility, stamina, bone structure, immune system—start to show their age, and need nurturing.

So, I offer ideas for slowing the decline, and maximizing the prospects of continued well-being. The five approaches, which I've already mentioned, are the following:

Activity	Both physical and mental
Looking ahead	Planning for the short- and long-term future
Independence	Self-reliance and control of your own life
Being of **V**alue	Doing worthwhile things for others
Empathy	Caring for and interacting with other people

These will be discussed in the ensuing chapters. Each is important enough to warrant a separate section. Please consider them thoughtfully, so you can plan your retirement life as carefully as you did your earlier years. It should be a long one—maybe longer than your career, and longer than your child-rearing years.

In addition to the above list, I have a second one, represented by the acronym, '4U.' It's just as important as the first one. As I said above, the first are what you should <u>do</u>, while the next suggests what you should <u>be</u>.

The four items in it are:

Understanding of Self	Self-knowledge and self-awareness
Understanding of Others	Insight into their needs and motivations
Upbeat-ness	Keeping a positive attitude
Un-rigidity	Flexibility and open-ness to new ideas

In considering this latter list, I stray dangerously close to psychological analysis. I try to avoid this, however, as well as sounding like a professional therapist. What I do is present ideas which have been advanced to me by such specialists, and describe my understanding of what I've been told. This second group is discussed at some length later.

You may question my saying that retirement should be a planned life. Theoretically, it's a time when you don't <u>have</u> to do anything. Yet all the evidence shows that drifting is a road to early decline. So, in building a new life for yourself after you quit working, you need a program for positive action. The concepts above are intended to give you a basis for doing this. I shall elaborate on them, and try to convince you how truly helpful they can be.

Acronyms for Living

"A.L.I.V.E." is both: 1) how we hope you'll be as long as possible, and 2) a reminder of what you can do to stay that way.

"A" is for "Activity"— (1) practicing physical exercise and exertion, and (2) doing things which require thought—both of these, every day of your life.

"L" is for "Looking Ahead"—cultivating the habit of always having some future event or activity in prospect, so that you look forward, and don't dwell in the past.

"I" is for "Independence"—doing things for yourself and making your own decisions.

"V" is for "Being of Value"—finding things to do for others which they will see as helpful to them.

"E" is for "Empathy"—caring enough for other people's feelings and concerns that you interact with them effectively.

"4U" represents 4 qualities I hope you'll evidence.

Understanding of self and others—insight into your own needs and motivations, as well as those of the people with whom you interact.

Upbeat-ness and un-rigidity—your basic approach to life, showing a positive approach and a flexible attitude, as well as an openness to new ideas and experiences.

Aging Gracefully

We see many old people we admire, and others we don't. What qualities do we want to emulate? How can we acquire them?

Many of the suggestions I make are intended to improve your skill in dealing with people, and your ease and comfort in doing so. They can help you become the kind of person you admire.

Everyone should think consciously from time to time about who he wants to be. To do this, you might want to create a description of the individual you'd like to be, especially as you get older.

I don't propose writing a detailed description, as you might if you were creating a character for a novel. But, you might make a list of words or phrases reflecting qualities you value in others, for example, consideration, politeness, concern, willingness to help, willingness to listen supportively, etc.

Start by taking one of these—one you believe you already possess—and observe yourself over a period of a month to six weeks.

Ask yourself such questions as: What did I do that revealed this quality? Did I miss some chances to show it? Could I have done better? What should I do to get better?

I don't want to sound like a scold, or preacher, or moralist. But I want to act on my belief that you, and everyone, want to be the best person you can be. As a retiree, you have the time to work on it.

It's easy to get in the habit of reviewing one's behavior occasionally—asking yourself questions like those above. I find that doing this helps me feel good about myself. If I think I'm getting better, hopefully, I'm aging gracefully.

If you become self-aware—recognizing your changing capabilities—and accepting them, you <u>will</u> age gracefully, and become the kind of old person every one admires and respects.

Habits to Avoid

I've already said that I don't want to sound like a moralist. I still don't, although it's hard to avoid when discussing harmful habits.

There's the unfortunate fact that little can be said that you haven't heard many times before. If the habit in question is part of your regular behavior, you've heard it over and over and over from family and friends.

What habits am I talking about? There are the physical ones—smoking, drinking, overeating, drug usage. And there are non-physical ones, like procrastination, competitiveness, laziness, bossiness, nosiness, perfectionism, and various compulsions.

Some of the preceding are habits of choice, some are addictions, and some grow out of a deep-seated need you may not understand very well. (I assume that you have at least one such habit. If not, congratulations! You're very rare.)

There is little I can say to change you, so I'll not try. I'll just sympathize with you as a fellow-traveler. I managed to avoid the physical habits—almost), but not the second group. I've been a lifelong procrastinator, competitor, and perfectionist.

But, I've reduced the intensity of all these three with psychological help, and none plagues me today as it did once.

I introduce this subject mainly to discuss the benefit of counseling. Although many persons feel that you must have a 'screw loose' if you choose to go to a psychiatrist, the simple truth is that a competent therapist—one with whom you feel comfortable—can help you examine any habits or tendencies about which you're uneasy. Over a period of time, this process can lead you to understand yourself better, and get control of your habits.

It's expensive, but it's worth it!

Chapter 8

Activity—(A)

Use It or Lose It!

I know the five principles I've proposed sound like stuff you've heard before. And of course, they are. Still, I doubt if they're matters that you've given a lot of thought to. Which is why I'm taking the risk of boring you with repetition.

And hearing them all before doesn't detract from their value. In fact, the truisms we hear constantly are repeated because they're usually both valuable and true. I know I promised to try to keep my material fresh, But, I also promised to try to keep it useful. Sometimes the two conflict.

The first suggestion I wish to make is:

Stay active!

I've stated that both physical and mental activity are important. This is a truism which deserves to be stated again and again and again. "Use it or lose it" is a quickie we've all heard, too, especially from people at the gym. And we know it's true. We know that unused muscles weaken and turn flabby, unused skills get rusty, and seldom-used thinking powers become reduced to thought mainly about day-to-day matters.

We have all read that physical and mental activity is key to a fruitful old age, and essential to extending one's lifespan. Following this chapter, I list ideas for doing this, dealing with various kinds of activity. I advance the value of walking, and consider ideas for mental activity. Right here, though, I'll limit my remarks to reasons why people don't do more.

We all know New Year's resolutions (like going to the gym regularly) frequently disappear in the short days of February (or even shorter days of January). We've all berated ourselves for not doing things we thought we should be doing. So why should it be any different once we become retirees?

Perhaps it <u>should</u> be different because our lives depend on it—in a way that wasn't true before. Perhaps it <u>should</u> be different because we have more time to reflect on it, plan it, and do it. Perhaps we <u>should</u> do it because so many people—family, friends, and helpers care about us, and hope we'll live long and happy years.

Whatever!

I was a teacher during my working days, and I learned early on that good advice rarely changes any one. I struggled, and my colleagues struggled, to motivate students—to get them to want to learn. Unfortunately, we usually had indifferent success. So I don't pretend that a few words on this page are going to cause you to change your ways. You'll have to do that all by yourself. But—you're reading these words (at least, I hope that much), which means that you have some desire to do something. And my comment is: "Hurray! Hold that thought, and let it grow!

I repeat:

Stay active!

Read on for some suggestions.

Activity—(A)

Activity implies 'action'—either your body is doing something with visible movement, or your mind is producing thoughts. Its inverse is 'drift,' where neither of these conditions exist, and life goes on without physical or mental effort.

Physical activity can range from such simple things as housework or walking, to carrying loads or doing heavy labor, to out-and-out exertion, like running distances and engaging in strenuous athletics.

Similarly, mental activity can have a wide range, from comparatively simple things, like Trivial Pursuit or charades, to more demanding challenges, like chess and crosswords, to still greater levels, like college courses or creative writing.

It's easy to say that you don't know what to choose, or that you'll start tomorrow, or that you have to get in shape first—or take some other delaying action. The simple truth is that there's no excuse for delay, even if you must begin at the lowest possible level.

If there's any doubt about your physical condition, you should ask your doctor about how slowly to take things at the outset.

As I've already said several times, I say again—planning is essential. You're not going to get any activity going unless you plan it and schedule it.

It's also essential that you not do anything you hate. If you do, you'll quit very shortly, and usually take a long time before you resume anything. There are too many options to allow this to happen—choose things you'll like.

It helps to have a companion in any activity you select. In games, of course, this is usually necessary, but non-competitive activities can become cooperative endeavors or friendly rivalries.

Physical Activity

Use it or lose it—strength, skill, agility, and stamina all dwindle unless utilized.

Some form of physical activity should be part of every day.

Walk! Walk! Walk! (At least three times a week, at least 30 minutes each time).

One way to get your walking in is to decide not to drive your car for any destination less than a mile away, unless you have something to carry, someone to take, or the weather is bad.

In bad weather (or any time), walk in an indoor shopping mall. Why not join an organized mall-walking group?

Get a dog who needs to be taken out for 10 minutes or longer two or more times a day.

Golf is an excellent way to combine walking, exercising, and socializing. Many people play golf well into their 90's.

Use stairs, instead of elevators, when going one or two floors.

Join a yoga class.

If you have problems with leg joints, you can sign up for an aquasize group (at the YMCA), or a tai chi class.

Think seriously about the exercise suggestions which appear in the following list.

Exercise and Exertion

Keep track—you should do at least 20 minutes of physical activity every day on as vigorous a basis as you can manage.

Learn how to take your pulse, and exercise briskly enough to maintain the pulse level your doctor recommends. Probably, you should raise it to 100 or higher—whatever she thinks is the right degree of elevation for you.

If you want to use a gymnasium or fitness center, that's fine. But if using exercise equipment bores or discourages you, don't do it. And don't think that buying equipment to use at home will result in your using it regularly—often, a piece ends up as a clothes rack. The gym, too, often becomes a wasted expense.

Try to avoid overdoing, e.g., don't lift anything heavier than 30 pounds (or whatever weight is right for you). Although, again, you should ask your doctor what's appropriate.

Remember, you're probably in your 60's at least when you retire, and you'll not be getting any younger. Moderation is the way to go—to keep yourself motivated and to keep yourself from getting hurt.

Be careful about running or jogging. It's easy to do damage, especially to your knee cartilage.

Also be careful not to try to do too many vigorous sports, or too much, like skiing, tennis, racquetball, long-distance hiking, flag football, etc.

If you have a balance problem, there are balance classes to help you.

If you become infirm, there are exercise classes which you take seated.

Walking

I've already recommended walking, but this activity is so important that I feel it needs further discussion.

Of all forms of exercise, walking is the most common, and certainly the safest—in terms of risk of injury or strain.

It's also the easiest to find opportunities to do.

However, the walking you do in the course of everyday activities, around the house, or running errands, shouldn't be counted, since it's too irregular, too unpredictable, and too sporadic.

You should plan (there's that word again) your walking. It's probably well to do it the same time every day.

If weather is a problem, you can use a treadmill, or walk at an indoor mall—many have groups that walk regularly.

Doing aerobic walking, in which you walk fast enough to elevate your pulse rate is not only good exercise, it also has the effect of building heart strength. However, it should be attempted only with the approval of your physician, who will suggest pulse-rate targets, usually starting at a lower level, and rising to higher ones.

Walking, like all exercise, is best done with one of more companions—going it alone allows for easy excuses to skip a day (and maybe another, and another, and another). Further, companionship makes the time pass faster and more pleasantly.

Even if physical decline limits many of your activities, walking remains one which can be practiced long after other forms of exercise are out of the picture.

Basically, I'm saying that you should take walking seriously. It may well be the principal means of maintaining your health.

Mental Activity

Perhaps, nothing delays the approach of the grim reaper as much as mental activity, regular and often. Many believe it also defers the onset of Alzheimer's, or other dementia.

Some possible activities:
  Crosswords and other puzzles.
  Board games—chess, checkers, backgammon, Pictionary, etc.
  Bridge, gin rummy, cribbage, and other card games.
  Teaching some one a requested skill.
  Mentoring or tutoring.
  Volunteering at the library, or tending a collection others use.

Various kinds of group activities:
  Book clubs.
  Group discussions.
  Courses at the local community college.
  Political volunteering.
  Committee participation (especially as recording secretary).

Reading! Reading! Reading!
In my opinion, nothing beats reading. Personally, I prefer non-fiction, but anything counts. I especially recommend reading a newspaper or newsmagazine faithfully. The only shortcoming reading has is when someone overindulges in it (as I have sometimes done) as an act of escape or procrastination, when something else really needs to be done.

Finally, there is writing. Nothing challenges the mind as much as putting thoughts coherently on paper (or the computer screen). It doesn't matter what you write, or who reads it—correspondence, letters to the editor, newsletters, stories, you name it. I particularly recommend writing your life story for the benefit of your children, grandchildren, great-grandchildren and friends. They would all enjoy knowing who you were, and what you experienced throughout your life.

Puzzles

I've mentioned puzzles above in listing mental activities. However, I feel this area needs more amplification.

I'm somewhat surprised that so many people seem so indifferent to them, calling them a waste of time, or simply saying they're not interested. Perhaps they feel puzzles remind them of the school homework assignments they once had to do, or maybe they reject them because they see no use for the eventual solutions.

A look at the local newspaper (in this case the <u>Denver Post</u>) shows the presence, in a single issue, of three crosswords, two cryptograms, one Sudoku, one anagram puzzle, one word riddle, one chess problem, and one bridge challenge. It's hard to see how, with this many and this variety, something can't be found to interest almost every one.

Of course, there are many more that appear elsewhere, including Arithmetic puzzles, Scrabble puzzles, logic puzzles, and a large variety of word puzzles.

Some of these enlarge your vocabulary, some improve your calculation skills, some refresh your knowledge of specific games, some sharpen your reasoning powers, and some simply rely on your love of language.

They exist at all levels of difficulty; for example, the three <u>Denver Post</u> crosswords are respectively easy, medium, and hard.

Since it's often difficult to find good mental activities, especially as one ages, I suggest that you make a systematic search among the puzzle magazine section in the supermarket, and try those which seem to fit your interests and ability. If you succeed, you'll gain an activity you can pursue well into your old age.

Learning

Of all the various mental activities, the one I feel needs the most elaboration is 'Learning," which justifies many suggestions I've made, like book clubs, group discussions, college courses.

Learning is a strenuous use of your mental powers, and one of the most rewarding—and it isn't limited to formal classes.

The old saying, "You can't teach an old dog new tricks," is NOT true; you can learn effectively at any age.

Useful learning activities can be as simple as learning to play a new game, learning the names of everybody in a group, or learning your way around a new town.

You can turn part of your regular reading into learning, by including serious writers on social, political, economic, psychological, or similar matters.

There are many learning opportunities between simple ones and formal classes. They include discussion groups, joint study groups (to look into topics of common interest), public lectures, and study at church, synagogue, or mosque.

Of course, there's always formal learning, as at a community college, which is not expensive, and is open to any one. Often, you don't have to work for credit, or take exams.

Some of the college courses to sign up for might include: (1) learning a foreign language, (2} managing investments, (3) foreign affairs, (4) home economics, (5) learning a musical instrument, or indeed, anything that appeals to you.

If there's a degree you always wished you'd earned, maybe retirement is the time to do it.

Finally, teach a class in an area you already know. There's no better way <u>really </u>to learn a subject than by teaching it to some one.

Writing

Writing is another mind-stretching activity which has already been noted, but which in my opinion needs further amplification.

It is perhaps the most flexible one you can use—wherever you are, and whenever you have a few minutes.

Of course, if you do all your writing on a typewriter or computer, you limit where you write, but there's nothing wrong with pencil and paper—many great writers have used this method.

Some people are turned off by what they see as the vast size of a writing project. But this need not be—there's no reason why a piece as short as a note to a friend, a comment on a recent occurrence, or a short essay or story can't be done.

The whole secret to successful writing is regularity. Even a small amount, like 100 words (a modest paragraph) a day comes to more than 36,000 words a year—already a book, though short. Writing a page a day yields a large volume in the same time.

It's been said that successful writing is merely the act of putting the seat of your pants on the seat of a chair. It may be hard to start this routine, but it can become a regular habit very shortly, especially if you start by sitting down at the same time every day. How do you think I got this book done—at age 94?

You can increase your pleasure by joining a writing class, perhaps at a community college. This can improve your skill, and teach you about editing your own copy. I think it was Ernest Hemingway who said. "There's no such thing as good writing; there's only good re-writing," (In describing that he produced some 17 editions of the first page of one of his novels.)

But re-writing is not necessary. When I wrote my own autobiography, I produced almost 500 pages, and then had it printed without revision. I just didn't care enough about the quality of the language to redo it.

Activities for Talented People

There's no end to any list of human talents: singing, dancing, acting, playing a musical instrument, art, photography, teaching, public-speaking—and I'm not even close to an end.

These are all performance, or exhibited, skills. I don't include the 'quiet' skills—scholarship, research, writing—or the talents seen in professional and vocational workers.

Persons able to perform in public (or private), or who can display their work, are a great asset to our society, and a special benefit to the world of retirement. They're able to keep constructively busy, they provide something which is valued by others, and their efforts help everyone socialize.

This is particularly helpful in the later years of retirement, when you might be living in a residence. Volunteering to perform, or teach something, or have an exhibit, is most welcome to individuals who don't get around much any more.

I've included public-speaking and teaching in this list of talents, although they seem a bit different from other performance arts. I do this because many older persons have stopped acquiring new learnings, in spite of their benefits. But they can speak or teach.

I suggest that anyone (and this means <u>anyone</u>—not just teachers) who possesses a skill, or area of knowledge, and is willing to share it, will find grateful people responding.

The possibilities are endless: sewing, knitting, crocheting, bridge, pool, other games, shop skills, a foreign language, current affairs, dancing, photography, painting, playing a musical instrument, or courses in history, geography, psychology, literature, the theater—these come to my mind as I write this.

Anything is possible; and benefits both the teacher and learners.

Chapter 9

Looking Ahead—(L)

Live in the Future!

If I had to give only one rule for longevity, it would be this:

Always have something planned ahead!

As I observe older people in a retirement residence, I notice that a very high percentage of them never seem to have anything to do (unless their family is visiting)—except what the social director has created. They look at the daily schedule to see what's going on, and don't seem to have an existence beyond this other than casual contacts with fellow residents.

How different from the typical life of an active worker, who has to keep job and home in balance, and cope with all the things which need doing. In this "real" world, one has to balance obligations and desires on a wholesale basis, and juggle everything.

Much of this carries over into the first few retirement years. Which it is why it's a good idea during this period to retain (or get into) the habit of keeping a calendar and schedule of activities. This habit will be extremely useful later on, as your life begins to slow. It will discourage any tendency to sink into lethargy, and let things just happen.

But, if you don't keep your focus on the future, you'll find your thoughts and conversation dwelling more and more on the past Not only does this make your conversation boring, it also tends to make you think your past is more important than your future. Dwelling endlessly on the past slows your activity level and thought processes. To me, it smacks of getting ready for the undertaker.

Having one or more activities always planned for the future, near-time or long-term, gives you something pleasant to think and talk about, and keeps your mental activity at a higher level. It focuses your life on what's going to happen, rather than on what's over and done. A continuing string of forward-looking moments will keep you alert and interested.

So. I'll repeat (in other words):

Always have something planned for the future!

Looking Ahead—(L)

Get in the habit of keeping an eye on the future, so you always have something to look forward to.

You can include such routine matters as doctor's and other health appointments, food shopping, visits to the barber shop or hair salon, tending to the car, doing the laundry, running errands, and the like.

But also include more memorable and pleasurable items, like going to the movies (but not watching them at home), eating out, inviting people in, accepting invitations, playing golf, tennis, etc., making dates for bridge or other games, scheduling attendance at classes and discussion groups, going to parties and social events, shopping in department and other stores, taking rides, going on picnics, and similar social and recreational activities.

The more you plan your activities, the more you're looking ahead, and the more you benefit from feeling you're in charge of your life.

Also, you improve your conversational practices. You have better things to talk about than your past life, your children and grandchildren, the weather, or current gossip.

Looking ahead becomes increasingly important as you age, since your mobility and independence become somewhat impaired, and you face the temptation to drift and let others do your planning for you.

When you wait for someone else to make your schedule and tell you what's planned, you tend to feel not in charge, and your sense of self-reliance and feeling of well-being decline.

Perhaps of all the suggestions I've made, looking ahead is the one least widely practiced—yet it clearly is one of the most crucial.

Keeping a Calendar

Essential to the task of keeping the future in mind is having a pocket calendar, and entering all dates in it. Be assiduous about this.

I suggest a pocket calendar because anything larger is likely to be left at home, be unavailable when you make appointments, and consequently be incomplete. I've found too that reminder cards filled out for you at professional offices are often mislaid or at least are not entered in the calendar.

It may seem foolish to you to write down, "Do laundry." or "Wash car," or "Go to the Post Office." But it keeps you in the habit of planning, and is comforting when you look at a full calendar.

In order to be sufficiently active, though, be sure that there are at least two entries for every week beside routine and repetitive matters.

It's important to write down the activity and time as far in advance as is feasible—this reinforces your habit of looking ahead.

If it seems unlikely to you that so much benefit can result from the use of a daytimer, let me remark that habit is curious thing. We often don't realize we're developing a habit until after it's well set in. Then, if it's undesirable, it's devilishly hard to get rid of. But good habits also tend to persevere, so if we develop a positive one, it can influence our life for a long time to come.

A pocket calendar also has the benefit of providing a place, which usually is with you, where you can jot down useful information. e.g., names and telephone numbers (if you don't have a cell phone), and facts about yourself that others can use in an emergency.

You can usually find a pocket calendar that covers a two-year span, so you don't have to transfer information annually.

CHAPTER 10

Independence—(I)

Hold Your Own!

With the topic, 'Independence,' I confront a problem I'll have to contend with throughout this volume. (And if you read it, as I hope you'll do, you'll contend with it too.) Almost all ideas I write about exist on a continuum. In the early days of retirement, something may not be much of an issue. At a later time, it can be crucially important.

My choice has been to introduce most concepts early in the book, even though many readers may feel they're not particularly relevant for them. But because of the continuum, it's not possible to say at what point they <u>will</u> become relevant. Further, the best way to prepare for the later years of retirement is to recognize at the outset what may be important later.

So—I'll start with 'Independence.' This is a difficult topic, since throughout retirement, you'll move from extreme independence to, possibly, extreme dependence. At every point, there will be a pull in two directions, as you try to decide how best to live your life. The area is ambivalent, because dealing with changes in how you're treated, changes in your lifestyle, and changes in your capabilities, forces you to make many adjustments—which might serve to undermine your independence,

Still, I urge you to follow the next principle. Indeed, I think it's vital that you do:

Be independent!

This may seem contradictory because I'll also speak about the importance of living within one's capabilities, and allowing others to do many things you need to have done. I make many suggestions for both in lists below. How can you be both independent and follow such advice?

The answer depends on how you define "independence." To me, it means the knowledge that you're in control of your own life, that <u>you</u> are making a decision to live within your capabilities, or to ask for to help—all without allowing others to decide <u>for</u> you. This determination to live in accord with your own ideas and needs is critical to a successful retirement and old age. No matter how old or infirm you get, it's still <u>your</u> life that you're living, and it's still your responsibility to decide how to live it.

I'm not saying you should be difficult to deal with. It's one thing to be independent, and not let others make decisions for you. It's another to be argumentative and stubborn, or aggressive and unpleasant. One of the great challenges in retirement is retreating gracefully from a state of total self-reliance to a place where you can be pleasantly independent within an ever-narrowing realm of alternatives.

Still, unless you experience a mental decline which prevents you from making rational decisions, it's a mistake to surrender your rights, and allow other persons to decide for you—where you should live, what you're capable of doing, what's appropriate behavior or dress, or how you should handle your money.

There shouldn't be much of this pressure in the first years of retirement, although some people do encounter efforts to influence them early on. But everyone will face this problem sooner or later. Friends and family think that they're concerned only about your well-being, and perhaps they truly are. But, they tend to base their suggestions primarily on your health and safety. They often don't place the same emphasis on your wishes and feelings. They may urge actions and decisions you don't like very much.

There's a real risk that you'll go along with some of this, since you know the others care for you and about you, and you don't like to appear ungrateful. But, the danger of going along too much is the likelihood that you'll begin losing your self-confidence, and start feeling you're no longer capable of doing much. This attitude can quickly start you on a downward path.

So, I say again:

Be Independent!

I append a few suggestions on how best to be both independent and self-reliant within a framework of growing older.

Independence—(I)

Do everything for yourself that you possibly can, although you should recognize when something is beyond your strength or endurance.

If others offer to take over responsibilities which you feel you can handle yourself, remember that the more you rely on them, the more you erode your feelings of competence. Politely decline.

When someone starts doing something for you without asking, explain how important it is to you to retain your independence and self-reliance, and say that you <u>really</u> want to do it for yourself.

If you do find yourself leaning more and more on others, think of new things you <u>can</u> do.

Errands, chores, laundry, and similar activities have the further benefit of helping maintain your physical fitness.

If you're in a group when a new challenge arises that somebody needs to do—don't be the last to volunteer.

Being independent doesn't require you to be stubborn, and insist vehemently that you still have all the physical capabilities of a younger person, nor does it require you not to give in gracefully when someone is absolutely determined to do something for you.

There's nothing wrong with hiring somebody to do something you find difficult. You're still in control of the act when you're paying for it.

Being independent becomes harder as you get older and your capabilities decline. Still, you should make your own financial decisions, schedule your own activities, and decide on your life style.

Self-Reliance

Independence is a frame of mind. Self-reliance is how you evidence this frame of mind in your everyday life.

It's not a determination to do <u>everything</u> for yourself. Instead, it's knowing what you're physically and mentally capable of doing, and not expecting others to do it for you.

Included in things to do regularly are laundry, cooking, household chores, paying bills, errands, grocery and other shopping.

When you can't walk or drive, you can take a van or bus or taxi. If you need someone to drive you, you can still do your own shopping and other errands. Plan to go to stores regularly.

Even if you're on a cane, or walker, or oxygen, there is much you can do, as millions of handicapped individuals have proven.

There are a many things which you should begin to recognize as beyond your capabilities, like heavy lifting, strenuous exercise, long periods of arduous work, or any extended activity calling for stamina.

For these, accepting offers of help should not damage your feeling of self-reliance, if you keep doing everything you <u>can</u> do. As the years go by, you'll have to rely on others more and more.

However, even in your advanced years, there are many things you can continue to do: household work, cooking (you may have to give up the stove), paying bills, driving (as discussed elsewhere), shopping, social activities, doing puzzles and games, and others. Fortunately, mental strength does not decline in the same way and same speed as physical strength (if it does, it becomes an issue I look at elsewhere), so you can show self-reliance in many mental areas, even as you're giving ground physically.

Living Within Your Limits

You may think that I'm writing out of both sides of my mind when I encourage you to be independent and self-reliant on the one hand, and advise you to live within your limits on the other.

The basic principle is to know yourself as realistically as possible, learning what is truly beyond your strength or endurance, or carries a risk of strain or injury, and what is not.

This is not easy to do, since we remember ourselves in our younger days, and we're tempted to try to do what we did then.

Not only are we older, with the losses of strength, stamina, and agility that the years bring, but we may also be badly out of shape, unless we've been exercising regularly while also working full time.

One way to treat your declining strength is to check it against a familiar suitcase. You should weigh the bag after you've packed it as you're used to, and then plan to lower the weight by five pounds every decade. This is probably an amount you can carry safely as you get older.

In addition to lifting, there are questions about speed and stamina—these should also be adjusted as you age. The time you need to walk a mile should increase by a minute or more, and the distance you walk decrease by at least a half-mile, every ten years. If in doubt, ask your doctor.

Although you probably won't do any damage by occasionally violating these standards, you <u>can</u> hurt yourself by doing so constantly, or to an extreme degree.

So, study yourself to discover what is reasonable and unreasonable for you; in so doing, you gain perspective on when you will need help.

Accepting Help from Others

Letting others help you may be one of the hardest things you'll have to do. You might see it as an admission of weakness or dependence, and you don't want to give that appearance.

On the other hand, there's the danger—if you get too used to having other people do things for you—of sinking into a pattern of over-dependence.

It truly is difficult, knowing when to accept help gracefully, and when to say that you need to do something for yourself.

It's easy to let somebody do things—because you're tired, or too comfortable, or it seems like too much trouble, or you're appreciative of the offer and want to be courteous. But you should resist, especially if the task is well within your capabilities, or an action you normally take.

As I said earlier, you should know your limits, and adhere to them conscientiously. And I repeat, a comment like "I really need to do everything for myself that I possibly can, for the sake of my health," should get the job done.

Knowing your limits, however, means there'll be times when you must accept help, or even solicit it. You have to be gracious and relaxed on such occasions. The essence of gracious acceptance is being cheerful and comfortable while someone is doing the job, and. especially, by not making suggestions or critical comments about how it's being done.

CHAPTER 11

Being of Value—(V)

Making Life Worthwhile

The recommendations I've already made, if followed, can do a great deal to help you get to be 100. But there's more! I have two more suggestions that I think will increase the probability you'll get the job done.

The next is:

Do something of value!

Perhaps the most demoralizing thing that happened to me as I aged was feeling that nothing I did made any difference to anybody any more. For years I was an active parent, raising children who turned out well (I think). I had a job that helped others gain knowledge and skill; I was active in many groups; and I got many things done. I felt I was a useful member of society, and had the satisfaction of sometimes hearing someone say, "Thank you," or even, "You made a difference."

But then came the time when none of this happened any more. My kids were grown, and living independently. I'd retired from both my profession and the various groups of which I'd been a member. Presumably, I was living the 'Golden Years.' In fact, little seemed golden about them. I scratched to find things to do. I found that bridge, travel, crosswords, and Sudoku weren't enough. What I wanted and needed was some one to ask my opinion, or ask me to be of help.

I discovered that writing my autobiography filled this gap to some extent. Family members and others had asked about my life, and seemed pleased when I said I was working on it. I found too that I could be useful by helping children who were having trouble in school. I learned that doing something another person found valuable was essential to my well-being.

I also realized that it was essential to <u>everybody's</u> well-being. As I thought about the nature of humans, and as I talked with people, I gained this insight. Everyone—and you who read this are no exception—wants to feel that he amounts to something. And amounting to something means more than just making more money, being endlessly busy, or retaining the skill to do things. It means hearing that one has been of help, or has done something to be admired. It led me to this admonition, which I repeat.

Do something of value!

In the ensuing lists, I not only deal with this topic generally, I also include suggestions about volunteering, tutoring, and mentoring, which are particularly effective ways of ensuring that what you do is of worth to someone else.

Being of Value—(V)

There are numerous ways to be of value—volunteering is one particularly flexible way, while tutoring and mentoring are especially valuable. These are discussed in ensuing lists.

Many organizations look for volunteers—some are detailed later, and suggestions made.

In addition, there are lots of less formal ways of being helpful. A few follow.

Take non-driving persons to appointments, or shopping, or on rides.

Take prepared meals to people who are sick or disabled.

Do baby-sitting, house-sitting, or pet-sitting.

Provide service in your church, synagogue, mosque, or other religious body.

Serve your neighborhood through membership on the board, or a committee, for your Homeowners' Association. Organize a Neighborhood Watch, or beautify public areas.

Share your experiences with a grandchild.

Visit lonely people, and be a friend to them.

Notice if someone is looking ill, or hasn't been seen recently, and, if needed, get help for him.

Volunteering

Volunteering is a formalized way to be of value—it usually involves working with one or more organizations.

The number of these with a need is beyond count. Among them are schools, hospitals, libraries, museums, charities, churches, synagogues, and other religious groups—even highway departments. This list, needless to say, is not exhaustive.

Some types of volunteering require specialized knowledge or training, or some measure of physical strength, and you should consider your capabilities in thinking about them.

You also have to consider such matters as how to get where you need to go, what out-of-pocket expenses you'll incur, how often and how long they'll expect you to be available, and whether you have the strength and endurance needed.

There are many benefits to volunteering, in addition to feeling of value. There's the change of scenery, the connections you make with people, your relationships with the persons you help, and the sense of vitality it all provides.

If you're looking for employment, organizations for whom you've volunteered can be a good place to start. They might offer full- or part-time work, suggest contacts, and/or give you recommendations and references—in any event, your experience there can be reported to prospective employers.

Among other things, you, yourself, will learn and grow because of the volunteering experience you've had.

Tutoring and Mentoring

Work in education is one of the most rewarding services a retired person can offer. I know how rewarding this work can be, since it was long my professional life.

Tutoring and teaching include the many ways in which you can work directly with students, among them are: 1) volunteering to be a teacher's aide in a classroom, 2) providing one-on-one help to children who are behind in school, 3) working in an adult-education program (e.g., teaching English as a second language, 4) teaching in Sunday-school or similar religious programs.

Of course, some of this work requires specialized training, which many of you have. For others, there are places which ask only that you be willing to teach what you know.

Mentoring is similar. Basically, it expects a person to share his experience with a young person preparing to enter adult life. Often, the latter needs only to know what to expect from a particular career choice and whether or not it is right for him. Persons from all walks of life may able to contribute in such a case. Mentors typically work with high school students.

Usually the contact is one-to-one, and frequently is on a weekly basis for a semester or a school-year. It's not demanding, and often leads to a lifetime relationship.

Possibly, the hardest part of providing any of the above services is finding the appropriate location in the first place. Inquiries can be made of school districts, charitable organizations, adult-education programs, and your local religious group.

Mentoring services described above differ from other volunteer work in that it's harder to quit, if you need to. You leave people in the lurch if you suddenly stop, and they're persons who need and count on what you're providing. It's important to try hard to complete whatever you agreed to do at the start.

Available Organizations

Above, I referred fairly generally to the kind of organization where you could be a volunteer. Now, I'd like to be a little more specific about ones in which you might be interested. You should offer your services only to one you admire, and feel attracted to.

All hospitals actively recruit volunteers, and assign them to such services as the information desk, the gift shop, and running errands for patients.

The need in veterans' hospitals is probably the greatest, since patients are usually there for a long time, distant from their families, and often with severe physical disabilities. They need everything—a listening ear, help in writing letters, being read to, a supportive human being. And we all owe them so much!

Then, there are the shelters, mainly for the homeless or for battered women (sometimes both)—they always need volunteers.

Countless charities, like Volunteers of America, Goodwill, Salvation Army, food banks, and many others welcome volunteers—you can deliver Meals on Wheels, or drive for the Red Cross. And there are lots more. I picked only a few of the best known, and include only those which provide services locally.

Local branches exist for many national and international organizations. If you have an interest in a particular cause, you can look it up on the internet (going to the library, if necessary), and find groups that have a local chapter. By contacting it, you may be able to serve a program that attacks a problem of special, and perhaps, personal concern to you.

Don't be reluctant to ask a librarian to help you use one of their computers. These days, when so much is best done on a web site, you're stymied if you don't know how to do this. Library personnel are exceptionally willing to help.

CHAPTER 12

Empathy—(E)

Love Thy Neighbor!

I come to the last of the five principles which I consider vital for preserving your life and health. I call it 'Empathy,' although I would rather have used the term, 'Interaction.' However, 'Interaction' would not have contributed to a usable acronym, and since empathy is an essential part of interaction, I use it instead.

In short, my advice is:

Empathize!

Since this term is not in as much current use as I'd like, I'll undertake to define it. Empathy is the almost instinctive or intuitive sense that you know what another person is feeling—where she's coming from. As Bill Clinton said, "I feel your pain."

This understanding of another is the essence of good human interaction. Once we get beyond superficialities, many conversations move toward matters about which we have feelings. As a result, things can be said or done that hurt, if empathy is not present—or help, if it is.

With other people, we can choose to do things in a positive way, or the opposite. We can support, compliment, and love, or we can complain, criticize, and condescend. Our treatment of them can be superficial, indifferent, hostile—or supportive and positive. It's all interaction, but the end-result is not always what we'd like. Everyone I've seen who's happy in old age operates in the first of these two ways, while most of the unhappy ones use the second.

You may ask why I'm making such a point of this. My answer is that all we really have in this life is one another. Humans desperately need other humans—nothing is more important than family and friends. Most of our satisfactions and dissatisfactions arise from contacts with people. If we get positive feelings from them, they contribute to our happiness and well-being. If we feel anger or resentment, or experience loneliness, our unhappiness grows and our health suffers. Good relationships make us feel alive, feel part of the human race, feel fulfilled. Withdrawal from others means that one is starting to die. It's as simple as that.

When World War II broke out, I was living in the Philippines. Shortly thereafter, my residence was changed to a Japanese internment camp, where I stayed for 38 months. It was then that I discovered how unimportant material possessions are, compared with relationships with people.

We need positive interaction to have a long old age. Christianity's Golden Rule, and the similar precepts of other faiths, all suggest that we should treat people as we'd like them to treat us. To do this we have to know that our feelings are also their feelings.

Empathy is essential to this. Our sensitivity to others, and our understanding of their feelings and needs bring us closer to them.

Therefore, I reiterate my advice to you:

Empathize!

The following lists suggest ways to do this, to socialize and interact, and to participate in group activities. I hope they're useful.

And now I've advanced what I think are the five keys to longevity. The rest of this little book is an effort to apply these principles in practical ways to your own life, so that you too can "live to be 100, or die trying."

Empathy—(E)

Empathy is the ability to be sensitive to other people's motives, emotions, and needs—to feel their feelings.

We should use this sensitivity in all our relationships. Whenever we interact with someone, we should be aware that we're either saying or doing things which might affect her.

Often, though, we're not aware of how the other person feels about what we've said or done, or what we've left unsaid or undone.

Learning to read expressions, and thinking carefully about what people say, helps us understand them better, and become more skillful at dealing with them.

All this is important throughout life, but doubly so in retirement, since the retiree may feel marginalized by society, and either concentrate on her own problems, or talk without thinking carefully.

One suggestion is to allow the other person to talk about items of concern to her, to at least the same extent you spend on your own priorities.

One way to improve is to ask yourself how you would have felt if the other person had said or done the same thing you just did.

Another is to ask questions in an area you know in advance is important to her, or which are designed to find out what she's interested in, or how well she's doing.

Etiquette, and books of manners, are just ways of codifying behavior which is sensitive to others. Be very careful about saying or doing things differently than they suggest.

All this is just common sense, which may be missing when a person gets hung up on her own feelings, thoughts, and problems.

Interaction and Socializing

Make friends!!!

Be truly interested (don't just pretend!) in what others say to you. Ask questions about what they're doing and what's going on with them—remember what they've told you when you're with them at a later time.

Recognize that staying in contact with people and sharing their interests (while resisting the temptation to spend hours at the TV, or on video games, or other solitary activities) is the closest thing we have to a 'Fountain of Youth.'

Look for opportunities to help someone accomplish something she needs help with.

Sign up for groups that interest you, and be sure to participate in any discussion or conversation that takes place.

Look for opportunities to take part in group exercises, games, social activities.

Be one of the helpers when an activity is being planned—setting up chairs and tables, greeting people, seeing if any one needs anything, answering questions, looking for loners, making sure others can see and hear, etc.

Organize groups for going out to dinner, or the movies, or sporting events, or just for watching TV or DVD's.

Be willing to work on neighborhood projects, or other community activities which will involve you with your neighbors.

Offer to baby-sit or pet-sit.

Reaching Out

Practice being the first one to say 'hello' when you meet someone.

Be aware if some one in your circle of acquaintances is unwell or injured, or having a bad time. Express concern, offer to help, invite her to dinner, or otherwise show your support.

If someone starts talking about a problem, be a "listening ear." Be supportive, without offering suggestions or stating opinions, unless asked—even then, be careful not to be too directive.

In a social situation, look for people who are not participating and open a conversation with them.

If you notice someone is not sharing in activities that others enjoy, talk to her, and ask if she'd like to take part. Don't push it, but if an invitation is all she needs, be the one to give it.

In discussion groups, be as supportive and appreciative as you honestly can about contributions of others, especially those of persons who seldom speak out.

If you drive, look for people who could benefit from a ride to the store, or to an appointment, or to the mall.

When you're running errands, or just going for a ride, look for people who would enjoy going with you. Or ask if you could run an errand for her.

Without trying to be an amateur psychiatrist, take note when some one seems troubled, and say something positive and friendly. Don't ask what's wrong, and don't intrude, but show you're a good friend who likes her and cares about her.

Value of Hugs

We don't do enough hugging in our everyday life, probably because we're uncertain if it would be welcome. Or perhaps we feel uncomfortable at this kind of physical contact with someone we're not intimate with.

Yet hugs—warm, friendly, innocent—send a surge of comfort through both parties. Physical, supportive contact tends to make participants feel a sense of human linkage and bonding which a handshake doesn't provide.

If hugging is hard for you to do, there are steps which might lead up to it. You can start by shaking hands with both hands, holding the other person's offered hand in both of yours, or using your second hand to clasp her arm or shoulder. You can graduate to placing one arm across her shoulders, in kind of a half-hug.

You can be more direct, and say something like, "I need a hug." With many persons, this will often result in one. If it doesn't, the whole matter can be dropped, as you move on to more customary conversation.

Many people seem to think that hugging is for women, not for men. Man-to-man hugs seem inappropriate to them, and man-to-woman ones improper.

This attitude seems to be declining, though, as we see athletes hug one another, and platform occupants in public meetings pass hugs around through both sexes.

Americans seem to do less hugging than people in other countries, especially Mediterranean ones. On the other hand, there are places, such as Japan, where virtually none of it is done. The habit seems to be culturally oriented, and we do what we're brought up to do.

Still, it's a comfort to many people, and could be for you too. Make an effort to become more of a hugger.

Group Activities

Any time two or more people get together (either planned or unplanned) to talk, or engage in a common activity (that is, to socialize) is what I call a group activity.

Such activities are critical to the continued well-being of the retiree, especially when the aging process becomes advanced.

There's a therapeutic quality about the contacts you have with other persons—the more time you spend alone, the more you sink into yourself, while the opposite is also true.

TV may be one of the most pernicious forces in hastening the aging process. It's always there, it's easy, it's comfortable, it doesn't require going anywhere or doing anything. In short, it beguiles you into a kind of lethargy which is not good for you—you should fight it!

There are so many things you can do in groups—playing games, having meals, walking together, shopping together, having a party, working on a joint project, participating in a book club or other special-interest group. The list is endless.

Try to do something in a group every day. Indeed, the more time you spend in some form of human interaction, the better for you. It's almost impossible to do too much, and few people ever come close.

While you're in a group, you're using, and hopefully improving, your empathic skill—the more you interact with people, the better you'll come to know them, and they you. The upshot will be more friendships and better human relationships.

Organize get-togethers for people to share ideas, play games, go to lunch as a group, or do anything in common which pleases them.

Friends

Everybody has friends, so what is there to say about them? Lots!

They're so important that I've created this special list about them. Their presence in your life may well be the seasoning agent which gives savor to it all.

Many people say they have lots of friends when they really have lots of acquaintances—friends are not necessarily the same as neighbors, fellow members of organizations, or fellow workers.

Acquaintances are people whose names we know, whose faces we recognize, with whom we pass the time of day, have conversations (even passionately and with contention), play games, socialize, but to whom we rarely reveal any secret corner of our being, nor they to us.

There are people in our lives, though, with whom we can say anything, knowing they care. Often, they're persons dating from our childhood or youth, with whom we can pick up a conversation after an interval of years, as though we'd seen them yesterday.

These are <u>friends</u>! And we never have enough of them—especially as we age, and travel less. So, my advice is to cherish those you have, and take special care to nurture them.

This may mean telephone calls, letters, visits and trips, endless listening to their problems, gifts and thoughtful acts— whatever! Do it! You'll never regret it, but you <u>will</u> regret failing to do it after it's too late.

If you're lucky enough to acquire a new friend, consider yourself blessed.

Having someone with whom you can discuss your deepest fears, dissatisfactions about yourself, or your most embarrassing moments can add years to your life.

Intergenerational Relationships

The title is a suggestion that it's good to have friends a lot younger than yourself—children, youths, and persons of active working age. Having younger friends will keep you younger.

There's stimulation from children, grandchildren, and others with an active lifestyle and interests different from yours. The only way you're likely to question any of your views is if you converse with people who don't share them. Spending time with members of other generations keeps you alert and vital.

All your life you've been in contact with people of all ages. When you were raising your children, you lived in multi-generational neighborhoods, you vacationed in places and attended social events with people old and young. This kept you flexible and current with events, even if you weren't aware of it at the time.

The best way to get exposed to new developments is to spend time with persons for whom they're part of daily life—cell phones, Ipods, Twitter, and whatever else is the latest innovation.

Your grandchildren grow up and move on, or away. Younger friends may spend more time with their peers, and less with those "out of the loop." Your free time often occurs when active people are working. In short, contact with many persons from other generations tends to dwindle.

It's only in retirement that relationships tend to become limited to persons of your own age. This makes it easy to become fixated on long-held ideas and habits, and narrows your life.

After retirement, and especially as you age, you should work at keeping contact with younger people. Your children and grandchildren are not enough. Try to keep at least ten percent of the names on your Christmas list those of younger friends.

If you have trouble keeping these friends, invite them to dinner, ask your son or daughter to invite them to a friends-and-family party, or celebrate a birthday or anniversary at a restaurant.

The Corrosion of Loneliness

Often, after you start living alone, and especially if you're in an apartment or residence, there are times when it seems easier to stay home than go out and do something,

Frequently, this period coincides with loss of a spouse, or other companion, so that grief may tend to erode any desire to go out or reach out.

It's important not to allow yourself to go into isolation. You'll vegetate, you'll lose contact with other people, you'll dwell on your sorrows, and there will be erosion of the skills you need for human interaction.

I often see persons in a retirement residence who have withdrawn. They seldom come out of their apartments, and seldom have much to say to anybody. Their response to greetings is perfunctory, and their replies to queries brief—in turn, they rarely make overtures to anyone else.

In my opinion, these individuals are no longer participating in life. They seem to be waiting for something to happen, although it's hard to see what this something can be, other than the inevitable end.

Regardless of your agreement or disagreement with the view I just expressed, it's clear that persons living a life of loneliness or isolation no longer receive the rewards which come from interacting with other people.

They no longer have the satisfaction of doing something for someone else, they no longer have the comfort of knowing others care for them, and they no longer enjoy the lift in their spirits which socializing can give.

It's no understatement to say that the end-result is a corrosion of the peace of mind and sense of self-worth which are so necessary to make life worthwhile.

CHAPTER 13

Understanding of Self

The Inner You

I'm now finished with the five principles intended to guide what you should do to reach 100 (hopefully). In this chapter and the three which follow, I concern myself with how to do what you do. Earlier, I distinguished between what to do and what to be. We're now at the what-to-be stage.

Everything which appears in the next few chapters, though, is just as applicable at any time of life as it is in retirement. However, the ideas are so important that I feel a need to include them at this time.

It's not easy to propose that someone make a basic change. It's one thing to suggest that he do something; He can decide to do it or not; and if he does do it, he can make a conscious effort to follow through—and may succeed.

But telling someone what he should be is a different matter. All of us are who and what we are, and change in our essential nature comes slowly, if at all. Such change involves both self-knowledge and determination, and often requires help from a professional advisor.

Knowing yourself is one of the most difficult tasks you'll ever undertake. Yet I'm asking you to try. It's crucial if you truly desire to have the best life possible. I'll discuss what's involved.

There are many ways by which we delude ourselves—and kid ourselves into thinking we do things for other than the real reasons. If you doubt this, watch someone you know very well. How often do you see him do something, and explain it in terms you know are pretense?

He may avoid going to the doctor, saying they're all fakes, when he's really afraid of what he might hear. He may skip exercise, saying it never did anything for him—but the truth is that he just doesn't want to. He decides to buy an expensive car, because "it will last so long that it will be cheaper in the long run." (REALLY??)

The world is full of choices a person makes for what he thinks are good reasons, but which, upon examination, grow out of a corner of his personality he hasn't examined. Over and over, we see people doing this—making a decision based on a motivation other than what they think is the real one.

It's easy to see people pretend—not just to the world, but to themselves. Indeed, it probably occurs more often than it doesn't. Seeing this so much, it should be hard for any of us to believe we don't do the same, at least from time to time.

I came to this conclusion about myself as I listened to my professor in a course on Mental Health I took in college. It resulted in my spending several years of early middle-age examining my feelings and motivations with professionals. Much of what I learned about myself came as a surprise.

I'm not recommending therapy or counseling for you, although I believe everybody could learn something useful that way. Instead, I suggest you at least admit the possibility that you don't understand all your motivations, and don't always know why you do what you do.

This admission is, I think, evidence of maturity, and a sign of personal security. It's only common sense to recognize in oneself what we commonly see in everyone else. Anybody who stoutly denies this is simply giving evidence of an ability to kid himself.

The following lists provide some thoughts on how you can look at yourself, and take steps to lead you to better self-understanding and its use.

Self-Awareness

Do you really, really know yourself?

We all think we do—we know our likes and dislikes in food and the items we purchase, we're certain of our preferences in cars, clothing, and furnishings, what we think of various behaviors. In short, we know what we'll decide most circumstances.

But we don't know as much as we think. I'll try not to sound like a psychiatrist, but I'll say that every one of us (me, too) does all kinds of things regularly without exactly knowing why. We often call them quirks or foibles or idiosyncrasies.

This isn't necessarily bad—indeed, it all adds up to what is called our personality. At the same time, it may include habits and tendencies which sometimes result in our saying or doing things we regret later.

While I don't recommend counseling to persons without serious problems, I do think you should examine your own behavior from time to time, in a manner similar to what I've already suggested for making health reports to your doctor.

We should reflect on our early lives—recalling events which caused us anger or tears at the time—to see if we still respond emotionally to incidents that resemble or remind us of them. Many such reactions have fairly simple roots in the past. Recalling childhood experiences can lead to understanding.

You need to note what was said or done, or what circumstances existed, immediately before an action you later regretted. By keeping a record of these and noting your recurrent reactions, you may gain some insight into why they irk you. Once you know this, you're in control, and can use this self-awareness to take charge of your habits. As I've said, this is incredibly difficult, and you shouldn't sweat it, but you can make it into a kind of game, to see if you can tease out bits of useful information about yourself.

Acting on Self-Awareness

Perhaps I'm getting too far afield with all this discussion of psychological matters. It's as if I'm producing a quick manual for how to understand people's personality and problems, including your own, and like every over-simplification, is full of chances for misunderstandings and misjudgments.

Still, I'm going to say something about how to act on the self-awareness you've presumably gained—even though it's possible that following my suggestions may lead to results you feel are not true of you.

"Fools rush in where wise men fear to tread" is appropriate here. Still, I'm going to forge ahead, since I make the assumption that anyone reading this book this far is serious about his life, and demonstrates a willingness and ability to look at issues squarely (or at least, listen). So, fellow-strivers—let's go!!

I've learned that not saying something I normally say, or not taking an action I've always taken, gives me a sense of self-control. If I don't react angrily when someone cuts in front of me, or I refrain from showing a person the 'right' way to do something, or I don't react to unkind comments—I have the satisfaction of knowing people have lost the ability to hold my feelings hostage to their words and actions.

If you do find yourself acting in petty ways over petty matters, you waste nervous energy. This saps it, and makes it harder to do other things you want to do.

Think about why you've been reacting peevishly in the past, and if you can't see a REALLY good reason to do it—don't keep doing it. Instead, look for more and more opportunities to exercise self-control. The more you do so, the calmer you'll feel, the better you'll understand your emotions, and you'll find yourself liked by everybody.

CHAPTER 14

Understanding Others
Know Thy Neighbor

It's paradoxical that understanding other people is easier than knowing ourselves. After all, we have access to our past history, our inner thoughts, and the fantasies and desires we hide from the world. Yet, we have trouble knowing the wellsprings of many of our own actions, even as we sometimes see clearly the explanation behind those of others—an explanation that they often do not perceive.

The two areas of self-knowledge and knowledge of others interact. Although we may look at the outside of human faces, and wonder what lies behind, we can frequently use our self-awareness to perceive where others are coming from. We can also use the insight we gain from watching them rationalize to see ourselves doing the same thing.

One way to gain insight is through study. It's unfortunate that more courses in Psychology, or Guidance and Counseling, are not offered in schools, or taken by students. I've already mentioned how a college class led me into a long program of self-examination.

Today, though, more people know more about human nature than ever before, and indications are that this trend will continue. Yet many persons of retirement age went to school or college before this trend took shape. It is to you that I direct my words.

Without attempting a two-bit course in Psychology. I'd like to say that much behavior you see that is hard to explain results from strongly-held feelings: anger, hurt, disappointment, grief, pain, self-doubt, among others. Jealousy, striking out (verbally or physically), defensiveness, slandering of others, aggressive criticism, bigotry, and many other negative words and acts have their wellsprings in these feelings. In order to understand the behavior of others, you have to discern the feelings that engender the words or acts you witness. In the first of the two accompanying lists, I give a few suggestions on how you might do this.

I don't pretend it's easy. Nor do I think you, or anyone else, will be a roaring success at it, just by following a few suggestions I make. None of us is a psychologist, especially me, and we cannot act like one. All I can do is report to you things that were told me by specialists, and give you my understanding of them. This may be imperfect, and my explanation may compound the imperfection. Still, trying is better than wringing hands.

Any progress you make will improve your effectiveness in dealing with people, as well as give you the satisfaction at knowing you have gained insight.

Gaining Insight

Although the accompanying chapter is called "Understanding Others," I've chosen to use the word, "Insight," in this list. I do this because I think the word connotes a sharper focus and a keener sense of awareness.

The first step in gaining insight into other people is to apply everything you know about yourself. If you're aware of what triggers certain responses in you, you can ask if similar responses from others can have similar causes.

Earlier, I suggested that you reflect on your early life, to see where some of your emotional responses originated. It's more than likely, the emotional behavior of others has similar sources.

We all know that undesirable ways of treating children and youths can leave scars in them. For example, numerous criticisms at a young age led me to the conviction that I had little ability and less likeability. For a long time, this crippled me socially, and led both to my being critical in my turn, and showing off when I'd done well.

Observing how children respond to various parental acts can provide you with much understanding. You can learn how childhood incidents can affect adult actions, and often, you can trace adult behavior back to its source.

When the source of a person's emotionality is unclear, noting what preceded his action should be accompanied by asking yourself why a certain type of incident might elicit a certain type of response.

When you do note what preceded an action you observe, it's often clear what somebody is reacting to. Many times, too, it's also clear <u>why</u> he's reacting—a putdown, criticism, condescension, or other attack has teed him off. Insight here is just common sense—but knowing <u>why</u> he feels so strongly, though, involves more knowledge about his background.

Using Insight

Insight into the words and actions of other people is the most effective tool you can have to deal with them effectively.

Again I say that I'm not trying to be an amateur psychologist, and I don't think you should either, although I <u>do</u> think everyone can benefit from reading and studying psychology from time to time.

Still, the more you understand where someone is coming from, and what her motivations are, the better you can tolerate her behavior. This explains the ability of mental-health professionals to maintain their equanimity when patients berate them.

This is similar to how we treat people in delirium or dementia, when they say or do hateful things. We take the position that they don't know what they're doing, and let it pass.

We should recognize that persons speaking or acting hurtfully are often unaware of the wounds they inflict. If we truly believe this, we can shrug off an incident—saying it's her feelings speaking, and she's not in complete control of her actions.

Unconstructive words may flow out of self-doubt, or wounded feelings, or unreasoning anger, or being in pain (physical or emotional). Once you realize what it is that distresses another person, you can cope.

I've found that if I know what's motivating someone, I'm more inclined to be compassionate and sorry for her than be angry.

Of course, there <u>are</u> people whose feelings are so deep-seated, and whose aim is so lethal in words or acts directed at others, that they're truly in need of professional help. Such persons are beyond the point where anything you can do will make a difference.

Chapter 15

Upbeat-ness

The Good Humor Man

I know you think the above title is weird. To the best of my knowledge, there's no such word as 'upbeat-ness'—or 'un-rigidity,' which appears in the next chapter. As I earlier noted, I created such words because I needed an acronym. In this case, I wanted one which started with 'U.'

Still, the area is important. Possibly, a better term is 'positive thinking,' although I find this to be kind of a 'blah' phrase, and one without any well-defined meaning. Another term I considered is 'affability,' and I've actually created a list of suggestions under that title. But it, too, doesn't ring a bell for me—lacking as it does in both impact and clear definition. It seems to connote a less intense level of upbeat-ness than I'm striving to depict.

In truth, I can't find a word which best describes the individual who has such a good attitude toward life that people bask in his presence—the person who you know will make the best of everything, lift the spirits of others, and generally enliven any group of which he is a part.

We all know people like this, and I for one envy them their happiness, their popularity, and their comfort with the stresses of life. And here I am encouraging you to emulate them, giving suggestions for you to follow; although I don't think I'm such a person myself.

Still, I know what the challenge is, and what needs to be done to get there. I too am striving, even as I suggest you strive, because I think the upbeat person is a good person to be.

I've written four sets of suggestions: 'Being Upbeat,' 'Affability,' 'Lifting One's Spirits,' and 'The Value of Laughter.' Together, I hope they provide some helpful clues. Even if you go only part way on the path to becoming a more upbeat person, you'll be welcome wherever you go.

Being Upbeat

Most people have a positive outlook much of the time. They've developed a frame of mind which is normal for them, and makes them reasonably relaxed and comfortable with other persons. Being upbeat for them is the end-result of efforts to lift their spirits, as will be discussed later.

But some individuals have such a sunny disposition that it fairly radiates—it warms everyone with whom they come in contact. It's this kind of personality which I wish to discuss.

I'm not suggesting that everyone can emulate such a one—a natural introvert can't convert himself into an extrovert. But I do suggest that anybody who wants to can elevate his personality to warmer and warmer levels.

How do you do this? Perhaps the first step is to try to be more optimistic. People are drawn to optimists (who expect things to turn out well), usually because they too want to believe, even if they're pessimistic themselves.

You can increase your optimism by noticing how things turn out in your life when there is a reasonable expectation either way. Take a look. If you find more positive than negative outcomes occurring, it might convince you to develop a more optimistic outlook.

People with a sunny disposition usually have a positive attitude toward other persons—they seem convinced others will be reliable, friendly, and dependable. Again, let me suggest you do a little research in your own life, to see how many of the people you know can be trusted, or trust others themselves.

If you accompany such a study with an effort to understand the persons in your life and discover why they do and say what they do, the number you think well of will increase, and your positive feelings will grow. You might even end by gaining, if not a sunny disposition, at least a sunny-ish one.

Affability

Affability is a characteristic we all recognize, but find hard to define. It's the nature of someone who's seldom aggressive or distant or upset, who's pleasant and friendly, and who doesn't get angry or offended easily. Maybe, the term, semi-upbeat, is apt.

Affability may not be the best word to use, since it isn't used much in normal conversation. Perhaps, it's better to substitute 'optimism,' 'positive thinking,' or even 'upbeat-ness,' when discussing this desirable approach to life.

It's not easy to be like this. Often, we're out of sorts, or stressed, or busy, or tired, when called upon to interact with others. If so, our discomfort may be revealed through indifference, inattention, curtness, or even rudeness.

How do you avoid such unpleasant forms of response, even though you don't feel like making the effort to be 'affable'?

Probably the simplest thing is to avoid social situations if you don't feel up to them at the moment, usually, there's no reason not to take a break if you need it.

When that's not possible, another alternative is finding something that needs doing—running an errand, setting the table, preparing something in the kitchen, and the like. Not only does this remove the need to interact, but the activity itself frequently makes you feel better.

Basically, being affable means giving yourself the chance to be your best self—taking an interest in others and their concerns. Since you're usually not out of sorts, you allow your natural impulse to like people to take over.

In brief, you practice some of the skills discussed in other lists—getting to know people, reaching out to them, improving your skills in social situations—and avoid being where you feel you can't be up to par.

Lifting One's Spirits

In the preceding list, I spoke about how difficult it is sometimes to be as affable as you'd like to be.

What are you to do, though, when you don't feel upbeat or affable, and you're forced to be in polite society anyway?

I've already mentioned busy-ness as a way to cope with such a situation. But busy-ness can do more than that—activity, especially physical activity, is a weapon for fighting depression, sorrow, disappointment, unhappiness and the "blues." Just a simple activity like walking, on a daily basis, may be the best way to keep your spirits up.

Exercise, doing chores, and other forms of exertion can do this too. You may not feel like any of these when you're low, but if you can force yourself to start, you'll reap a benefit.

Reading, doing puzzles, playing games, even video games, serve similarly. The whole idea is to start doing something that directs your attention elsewhere than at your sour feelings.

What you <u>don't</u> want to do is dwell on your thoughts and hurts, or sink into some kind of lethargy—although napping can be a help, if you're able to drop off.

In brief, lifting your spirits is fundamentally a task of getting back to normal. I assume your normal attitude is one of acceptance of life—a positive frame of mind. When you're out of sorts, this has been disturbed, and the disturbance needs to be removed. If you find yourself chronically unable to do this, it's a sign you may have a deep-seated problem, and you need counseling.

The Value of Laughter

Perhaps I'm spending too much time trying to turn you into a Merry Andrew and suggesting ways to cheer you up. Still, I'm convinced that positive thoughts, attitudes, and behavior are conducive to health and long-life.

I was first convinced of this when I read Norman Cousins' 1979 book, *Anatomy of an Illness*, in which he described using laughter intensively, with the help of comic films and similar materials, as a tool to fight against the pain and progression of an illness his doctors thought terminal. Instead, he recovered.

A number of books have been written over the years similarly trying to draw a connection between a person's frame of mind and his ability to stay healthy, or to return to health when sick.

Regardless of your opinion of this thesis, it surely can't hurt to engage in such a lighthearted and happy thing as laughter. Even if it has no impact whatsoever on your health, it can at least impact your good spirits and enjoyment of life.

Some people try to avoid laughing uproariously, or even loudly, thinking others might find it unpleasant. I suppose this can be true of a person who hoots at his own unamusing jokes, or who laughs excessively at what no one else thinks is funny. Still, most people are drawn to someone who enjoys humor to the hilt, and they laugh along with him.

In short, I encourage you to hone your sense of humor—go to funny movies, or bring them to your DVD machine or VCR. Watch comic shows on TV, or if you can't find them, re-run some of the great ones from years past. Read humorists, take note of hilarious stories you find, and share them with others.

We don't laugh enough—we need to laugh more, and be open about it. In particular, if someone says something funny, show your appreciation with a whole-hearted laugh. You may extend your own life and help others to do the same.

Chapter 16

Un-rigidity

Forever Flexible

Again, a weird title appears—this one weirder than the last. The things I go through, and put you through, stretches good sense to the limit! Still, if it helps you remember, it's done its job.

Of course, there's a better word than 'un-rigidity'. The word is 'flexibility.' And it's about flexibility that I direct my comments.

We all like to think of ourselves as flexible. The simple truth is that we're more addicted to patterns and habits than we like to admit. From eating the same thing for breakfast every morning, to taking the same path to work regardless of traffic, to staying with familiar brands and products in the supermarket, to countless other routines we follow without re-thinking them—we fill our days and nights with repetitive practices that make us feel comfortable.

There's nothing basically wrong with this. It may well be that for some people, especially at certain times, it really is the best way to go. Still, it doesn't hurt to review one's lifestyle occasionally—to see if other ways might be an improvement.

Doing this is more important in retirement than at any other time. The ease with which you can slip into comfortable patterns is greater than in your earlier, more active life. Without urgencies in your days, you can readily find yourself living in little patterns. And if your strength or health begins to weaken, the trend is intensified.

But things do change, even in your later years, and you should try to change with them—at least a little. Going from a typewriter to a word processor is one example of something you should do. So is using a cell phone. Don't fall into the habit of calling all new things too difficult to use. ("And who needs them anyway?") My father bought his first automobile when he was 68 years old, but refused to learn to drive it—and for the rest of his life had to rely on some one else (mostly, my mother, who was younger) to take him places. I felt then, and I feel today, that he made a serious error.

Older people are notorious for fixating their habits for the rest of their lives—especially if they've lived alone for any length of time. I see many of my fellows whose life patterns are so predictable that I know where I can find them and what they'll be doing at any particular time of the day.

My point is that although this approach is comfortable, it tends to reduce the amount of mental activity we do, and may reduce the amount of physical activity as well. It's generally accepted that the more we use our thought processes, the more we're able to defer our mental decline. So, inflexibility is something we should avoid.

Thinking about what to do next, and whether to do something different, or even the same thing differently, keeps us alert and mentally alive. Why not vary the time you eat breakfast, or any other meal, if it's possible? Why not change the time you take your walk, or do your laundry, or go shopping—if for no other reason than to avoid sinking into a rut? Why not watch some new television programs to see it you like them? Or say hello to some people you haven't met yet? Or learn something new—cooking a new dish, reading up on a current social, political, or economic issue, or even learning a new board game?

Of course, we all do some of the things I'm suggesting. But we also have a longer list of things we do in patterned routines. If you take the trouble to make an actual list of everything you do at the same time and place every day or every week, you might be astounded at how much there is. You might even be encouraged to change.

The number of new things to try, or old things to do differently, is endless. It's limited only by your imagination, energy, and willingness to experiment. You may find, though, if you make the effort, that you've added zest to your life, and increased your chances of living longer.

Now I've reached the end of Part 2 of this little book. In the next part I consider a number of issues which arise in the stage of retirement that follows your vigorous early years. It deals with what concerns many people, namely, how to handle the many life adjustments necessitated by inexorable changes in your capabilities.

I hope the eventual outcome 4U will be
that you are ALIVE at 100!

Flexibility

Repetitive, unchanging behavior is one of the most insidious pitfalls we can get into, because it encourages us not to think.

Whether we eat at the same restaurant all the time, do the laundry only on Monday, buy almost everything at Walmarts, or think of Saturday as movie night, our lives are organized into patterns.

We do this because it feels comfortable and it's easy, and we don't have to do any special planning (i.e., thinking). We often continue the same way even when changed circumstances show that something different might be beneficial.

During working and family years, emergencies, special needs, and unexpected events keep patterns from taking over completely. During retirement, many of these variables dwindle or disappear, and the likelihood of repetitive behavior increases.

Older people are notorious for being set in their ways, especially if they've been living alone for any period of time. It's vital that you keep this possibility in mind and strive to avoid sinking into rhythms and repetitions.

We have enough of these inevitably, with meal hours, payment deadlines, and scheduled events—so we should do our best to be flexible in as many other areas as possible.

Variation in menus, walks (when and where), activities (time, place, and choice of what to do), investigating new TV programs, making new friends, shopping in new areas—the list is endless for new things to do and new ways to do old things.

You will need (and I hope, want) to avoid rigidity, because sinking into ruts is truly <u>sinking</u>. It leads to fewer and fewer times when you do planning, and it leads down the road to doing more and more of the same things more and more often. Loss of flexibility can be thought of as the early onset of rigor mortis.

Open-ness to New Ideas

Those who are open to new ideas are certainly flexible, but the reverse is not necessarily true. It's possible to be flexible in scheduling or consenting to familiar activities, without looking for new ones.

One indicator of how open you are to new ideas is your use of technological advances like computers, cell phones, and PDA's. If you're not familiar with any of these, ask a knowledgeable person to give you a quick look at their uses.

Another indicator is whether you've changed your mind, or even investigated a differing point of view, on any political, economic, or social question.

Open-ness can mean reading, or listening to, commentators from both the liberal and conservative sides on issues you care about.

It also can mean making a conscious effort to learn something. (In an earlier discussion of mental activity, I included a section on "Learning"). This is the epitome of being open to new ideas, since by definition it means acquiring knowledge or skills you don't already possess.

There are still other ways to gain or demonstrate a readiness to embrace new ideas.

You can engage in meaningful conversations with acquaintances with varying backgrounds, in order to learn more about their areas of expertise.

You can participate in a group, or if necessary, organize one, to exchange views about current issues which concern you.

Also, you can ask questions about other peoples and cultures from members of those groups, or from people who have lived abroad, or traveled extensively.

PART 3
- *The Home Stretch* -

Second Adulthood

Until now, I've concentrated on matters of interest and importance to the newly retired, and those in the so-called Golden Years. But new retirees eventually become longtime retirees, and many of their earlier needs and concerns undergo alteration.

For example, in the later years of retirement, you will either have already made a decision about housing for most of the rest of your life, or you're in the process of doing so. You will have begun experiencing some of the aches, pains, and physical debilities of advancing age. And, you will have made many changes in your habits and activities.

I call this time, after the long period of vigorous retirement, 'The Home Stretch.' I'm not sure this is the best name for it, but I can't think of a better one. It endures from the point when you first begin to sense a need to retrench to the moment when you're forced to acknowledge that simple daily living will require assistance. Perhaps I should call this section, 'Later Living,' or 'Life Changes,' or 'Staying the Course.'

Part 3 of this little volume is concerned with this stage of your life. In it, I try to anticipate questions and conditions which will arise, and suggest ways of dealing with them. I've found ten areas I consider to be of importance, and dedicate a chapter to each, with one of more lists. Since I'm now in this period of my own life, I speak from a large amount of recent experience.

CHAPTER 17

Changing Family Relationships
Yielding Authority

It's often said that families start out with parents as parents and children as children, and end up with parents as children and children as parents. This recognizes that as people get older, and less and less involved in the busy-ness of the world, their children, who are immersed in this same busy-ness, tend to make more and more decisions on behalf of the parents.

It's natural to do this, especially if the older persons are living a quieter, more circumscribed life, with waning physical and mental powers. Frequently, such parents have turned over control of their property and possessions, to relieve themselves of the continuing burden of responsibility.

Even when such a transfer has not occurred, though, and even when the parents' lives are still quite active, and their capabilities still strong, children are somewhat inclined to believe they know what is in the best interests of Mom and Dad—better than the parents themselves. In brief, after people retire, and start the unremitting process of the rest of their lives, there also starts a changing dynamic in their family relationships. I consider this change, and what to do about it, in my present remarks.

I've already mentioned how people are treated differently once they enter retirement. Changes in family relationships reflect these broader ones. The parents are seen as no longer fully participating in the active world, and increasingly, their views are seen as outdated.

But, there's more to it than that. Within the family, more get-togethers are at the home of a child. Increasingly, family conversations center around the activities and concerns of the younger generation; and family activities and excursions are often seen as too difficult for the parents to participate in.

More and more, too, the parents are asking for help—help moving, help getting places, help with decisions, help with modern technology. And more and more, the children or other family members insist on helping.

This changing family dynamic is doubtless different for every one. The vigor of the parents, the proximity of the children, the size of the family, the established lifelong relationships —all these make their contribution to how things develop.

So, I cannot generalize too greatly. What I <u>can</u> do is offer a few suggestions for you to think about, and possibly try out.

Changing Family Relationships

Don't expect that there won't be changes. Many are caused by the attitude of the working society toward those who have quit, while some come from the belief of younger family members that their lives demand endless decision-making, while you've moved into a different world.

In particular, you should realize that the days of your parental authority are long gone. Once, your children leaned on your judgment—now, they expect you to lean on theirs.

Know that family members may be concerned about your having enough money to last your whole life. Don't be surprised if they raise questions about expenditures which might affect your future security.

Part of this concern lies in their feeling that if you run short of money, they might have to be responsible for your well-being—and this could come at a difficult time in their lives.

Probably, you should make it clear that you love your family, will do anything you can for them, and listen to their ideas and suggestions, but that as long as you have mental ability and financial resources, you'll make the final decisions on how you'll live your life—especially if this doesn't impose a requirement on any of them.

Recognize that the actions your children take are based on their love and concern for you. However, as with professional care-givers, their conscious attention is placed on tangible matters they wish to influence, like your health and safety. They may not always be aware how you really feel about things they do or suggest.

The love and support of an extended family should be a great joy to you, and nurturing it will go far to help you live a long life. This is in spite of the ambivalence of the preceding statement.

Dealing with Your Family

One hears, "Be careful how you treat your children, they'll choose your nursing home some day."

Inevitably, sons and daughters try to influence the decisions of their retired parents—they push them to stop driving, they tell them to slow down and not do too much, they urge them to enter a residence, they make financial decisions for them. Listen nicely, but reserve the right to make up your own mind.

Make it easy for a younger person to be helpful, by soliciting his opinions and assistance, and admiring his accomplishments.

Don't offer unsolicited advice about child-rearing, householding, finances, or anything. I know it's unfair that your children can feel free to advise you, and you can't do the same to them, but we all know that life is not fair. They'll say in their defense that the situation was reversed when they were young.

Making your own decisions, particularly when they go against their recommendations, can result in conflict with family members who are convinced they know best. Yet, you're the one who should decide where to live, when to stop driving, how active to be, and how to spend your money.

Unless you're truly loaded with assets (or maybe, even if), major financial decisions should be made in consultation with your family, and their opinions and recommendations considered carefully. Still, your views are the more important, and, if the others fail to persuade you, should prevail. But be reluctant to insist on your rights in the face of universal resistance.

When a young person wishes to marry, he usually seeks his parents' approval—when he gets older, though, he may feel he needs to ask his children's permission. A late-in-life marriage, though, <u>should</u> be a family decision, if only because of the financial and legal issues. If you marry in spite of opposition, it could damage your family relations, and possibly lead to later problems.

Living with Your Family

Family relationships get more complex if it becomes necessary for a retired person to live with one or more relatives.

Frequently, this is occasioned by financial need—if the older person runs out of money (often because of major medical expenses), moving in with a family member may be necessary.

While it is legally possible for a relative to decline financial responsibility, and thus force the government to support an indigent elder, most loving sons and daughters are reluctant to do something so rejecting.

Other reasons may exist for taking an older family member into one's home, most notably, the desire to provide needed care in a manner difficult to find in an institution.

Some people feel strongly that aging parents and grandparents need to be sheltered in a loving family, and live out their days surrounded by children and grandchildren. This is standard practice in some cultures, notably in the Orient, where multi-generational families abound.

Many issues can arise when a retiree dwells in a family home—there may be conflicting views on raising children, the retiree may interfere in the running of the house, there can be an impact on the social activities of the younger persons, who don't want to exclude an older family member, but don't feel he fits in comfortably either.

If the retiree has several children, there may be a question as to how the responsibility will be shared, including the costs, and if anyone feels he is carrying too much of the burden.

Tensions can occur in living closely together—maybe difficult to resolve. At the time a living arrangement is begun, an effort should be made to anticipate such problems, and reach an agreement on how to handle them.

CHAPTER 18

Retirement Residences

All-in-One Package

Some time during retirement, the question will arise about moving into a residence. The age at which this might occur varies widely, as will the age at which the actual entry might take place. Some persons enter a community before they're 60, while others wait until much older. I myself moved into one shortly after my 91st birthday. Many people never enter at all, and live independently, or with a family member, or otherwise, all their lives.

On the next pages, I present some of the pro's and con's of this kind of living, and how to evaluate a particular location. I also make suggestions for living in one. But, I'd like to make one or two general comments at this time.

Retirement residences have a number of things in common. They all offer room and board, some kind of emergency health care, transportation, housekeeping services, and a variety of planned activities. For this, the level of payment is considerably higher than it would be for a comparable apartment elsewhere, plus eating at restaurants. The additional cost can be viewed as payment for the activities and services provided, plus a kind of insurance against a possible need for emergency health assistance, or for assisted living or nursing care at a future time.

Since the details of what a given place offers differ from location to location, it's necessary for you to understand exactly what you're paying for at the time you choose a place.

You should also think about the changes that may occur in your way of life, other than those you'd expect any time you move into a not-very-large apartment from a roomier dwelling—the most common circumstance.

You'll be living in a place a little akin to a hotel, and a little akin to a college dormitory. There will be public rooms (including a dining room), in which you and your fellow residents often meet, either one-on-one, or in groups. There will be large numbers of persons using canes or walkers, and/or oxygen, creating some of the feeling of a convalescent home.

I hope I'm not being unfair or biased in these comments. What I'm trying to do is describe the conditions which typically exist, so that anyone moving into a residence is not surprised. These communities are certainly acceptable at a particular stage of life, and may even be necessary. Still, the institution constitutes a major change in one's circumstances—a greater change than you may fully realize in advance.

You may ask if there's anything between apartment living and retirement residences. The answer is, Yes. There are senior apartments which have been created with the needs of the elderly in mind. These come with all degrees of amenities—from those with little more than a lobby where tenants can meet, to places with almost all the services of a residence.

However, there is not usually a restaurant on the premises, nor a nursing service, nor a large number of organized classes and activities. There may be a van for transportation, and there may be some way of keeping an eye out for your well-being and answering an emergency summons—and there may not.

You have to be capable of a high degree of independent living to consider a senior apartment. But if you are, and you're very mobile, one may be right for you. Certainly, it's a less expensive way to go than a retirement residence.

I try to make specific suggestions in the lists that follow.

Retirement Residences

Pro's

There are people you can call on, 24-7, if you're ailing. There are also persons who can help you with other problems.

There are many fellow residents to interact with.

There's a wide variety of group activities in which you can participate.

You don't have to do cooking unless you want to, since lunch and dinner are available in the dining room—often, breakfast, too.

You have a regular cleaning and housekeeping service.

If you no longer drive, or don't want to, there's a community van.

Your family and friends feel assured that you're safe and tended to.

You have some protection against the future problems of old age.

Con's

Most of the disadvantages of apartment living apply here too.

The cost is high, and you may not use all the services you pay for.

The transportation provided may not meet all your needs.

If the place becomes unsatisfactory, moving may be difficult, and at a difficult time of your life.

Seeing many people on oxygen and walkers can remind you of your own mortality.

It's uncomfortably easy to sink into a kind of lethargy.

Having guests or entertaining is often hard to do.

Choosing a Residence

Visit at least once without a prior appointment, or prior notice.

Talk with current residents, not selected by a staff member, and not under any one's watchful eye, to ask what they like and dislike.

Observe the premises, taking notice of cleanliness, needed repairs and maintenance, and availability of facilities which are important to you, such as exercise room, library, arts & crafts room, extra storage space, parking arrangements, etc.

Examine carefully the kind of living quarters you are thinking of occupying—apply the above criteria, with particular attention to bathroom facilities, kitchen adequacy, storage, and how your furnishings would fit in.

If you want to be particularly careful, measure the rooms, reproduce them in a scale drawing, and do the same with your pieces of furniture, so you can see how they can be arranged.

Ask about accessibility to shopping, restaurants, and traffic-free walking areas, as well as the kind of transportation provided for residents, what it can be used for, when it's available and how it's scheduled.

Eat a meal in the dining room, and ask one or more residents if it's representative of the typical fare.

If the facility is not operated on a non-profit basis, ask for the record of recent price increases. Ask some residents if they view the increases as fair.

Observe personnel, seeking to ascertain their concern for residents, and how they interact with them.

Consider selecting a residence which provides assisted-living, as well as independent living, in case of later need.

Life in a Residence

Once you enter a residence, you make a major change in your lifestyle, and you must build new patterns of living.

If you're still quite active, and especially if you drive, you can live much like in an apartment—you get out when you need to, and you can have many activities away from the residence.

But, if you can't do this, you need to adjust to the rhythm of life in the facility, and use the amenities and services it provides.

These typically include: the dining room, lounge, library, exercise equipment and classes, bingo and games, scheduled get-togethers and outings, regular movies or entertainment, meetings of all kinds, van service, housekeeping visits, and emergency health care on call.

Because so much is provided, it's easy to become over-dependent, and let life just happen. It's essential that you keep to your regular physical activities, and continue to plan for the future.

But you may have to make changes—you may replace walking with exercise equipment, if getting out is difficult—and future events you plan for may have to be inside rather than outside.

Still, your life is in your own hands, and you can retain control of it. You must continue to do as much for yourself as possible—this is even more important after you enter than before.

Once you enter a residence, it's rare that you will live again outside an institution! You have to adjust your thinking, and consider what the rest of your life will be. You have to choose activities which you truly enjoy, and can continue to pursue—with diminishing physical powers—in a self-contained environment.

Treasure your outside contacts—they give you an unparalleled opportunity to do things outside the residence.

Senior Apartments

The term, 'senior apartments,' is not typically seen in directories of senior services. I've chosen it to describe a building or complex which offers some amenities for seniors beyond what is normally provided to apartment dwellers.

These amenities can vary—frequently offered is a manager with an interest in seniors, and the ability to help them find local resources they might need. Also, units may have a call button or chain, to summon help in an emergency.

Less often found: van service, exercise room, social room, restaurant, swimming pool, or what have you?

Rents for senior apartments are usually fairly comparable to those for apartments generally.

The advantages and disadvantages of all apartment living of course apply to senior apartments, which have been set up as a compromise between an apartment and a retirement residence.

Senior apartments are hard to find, since many listings put them in with apartments generally, and others intermingle them with retirement residences. It takes a little doing, looking on the internet, or in the newspaper, or getting help from a senior resource center or advisor.

If you feel you're not ready for entering a residence, but at the same time want a little greater sense of security than you can get in a regular apartment, then a senior unit is the thing for you.

Many times in such a place, a lot of social contact takes place among the various tenants, resulting in positive life experiences you don't normally find in an apartment complex.

Chapter 19

Driving

Giving up the Keys

Driving a car is considered almost an inalienable right by many Americans—even though the government publicizes the fact that legally it's a privilege which must be earned, and which can be taken away for cause. We usually get our first license in our teens, and by the time we reach retirement age have been driving for over a half-century.

Certainly, there's no issue in this connection for the vast majority of retirees—in the early years. But early years turn into later, and then still later, years. And every one who reaches an advanced age sooner or later hears suggestions that maybe it's time to surrender the car keys.

New retirees have much more urgent matters to deal with, though, and they view this issue very much as they earlier viewed retirement itself—something to deal with in the far future. Nonetheless, like retirement, there's a benefit to looking forward, and not being caught unaware or unprepared. I'll speak to this from my own experience.

At 93 I was still driving, and considered myself to be competent. Of course, I understand this is what all older drivers believe. I'm told that they're the last to see and admit their deficiencies, and they're usually not as good as they think they are. And, I experienced some of the problems of old age, I had trouble seeing the curb at night, and sometimes bumped it, especially on right turns after coming to a stop.

Then, if I was not concentrating as hard as I ought to, I found myself veering a little to the left, not enough to endanger traffic, but enough to irritate myself. After all, holding a straight line is the hallmark of the efficient driver, and this made me wonder if I really was as competent as I thought.

You'll notice that the last two paragraphs are in the past tense. Since I had my stroke in November of 2009, I've given up driving, at least until I regain strength in my right hand and leg, and can pass a road test.

So, what I shall be doing at some point in the near future is scheduling a road test. In fact, I think all older drivers, probably everyone past 70, should have this test every two or three years. If you do this, you can avoid tensions with your children over whether you're still safe on the road, and can refer the matter to a qualified professional.

I've learned a couple of things about senior driving. The first is that it's easy as you get older to let your attention wander, and when you do, you place yourself and others at risk. So, the older you get, the more you must stay focused on the task at hand, and the more you should resist any habits of looking around and checking things other than the road.

Also, you should drive defensively. This of course is true of all drivers of all ages, even though I observe many, if not most, of the cars on the road being driven otherwise. I recall a conversation I once had with my mother many years ago, when I was commenting on something she did behind the wheel. "Clifford," she said, "I'll guarantee to you that if I have an accident, it won't be my fault." My reply was, "I'm trying to guarantee that I won't have an accident, period."

This is the classic difference between defensive and other drivers. The latter, if they're law-abiding and conscientious, try to follow the rules of the road, and expect others to do the same. The former anticipate that other drivers may well break the rules, and they seek to position their vehicle in such a way as to avoid collision if this occurs.

I've often compared defensive driving to the way a person should handle his car on an icy road. He should look ahead as far as possible, to anticipate the moves of others, and should brake, turn, or accelerate with moderation, so as not to have to take action on a sudden basis. For example, when passing close to pedestrians, bicyclists, or parked cars, the driver should be prepared for someone to turn suddenly, or a person or animal to appear unexpectedly, and not be caught by surprise if it occurs.

Perhaps I've spent too much space on defensive driving, but I do so because it becomes more and more important as you age. Your reflexes inevitably slow as the years pass, so your ability to react quickly diminishes. You can offset this to a great degree, though, by developing the habits I've just discussed. In this way, you can defer almost indefinitely the day when you'll have to surrender your car keys.

I present this discussion in a book to be read by you as a new retiree, because it's never too soon to start exercising the thoughts and developing the habits which will protect you through a long retirement. In today's world, the loss of the independence attendant upon giving up driving is so hard to accept, that anything that can be done to keep it in the future is worth trying.

I add a few ideas in the ensuing list. I also add thoughts about how to handle matters when you do have to stop driving.

Driving

Driving is an important part of your sense of independence, so you should strive to drive competently as long as you can.

In the early years of retirement, your driving experiences will be about the same as they've always been.

Being able to drive as you get older is more and more of an asset as others start giving up their cars, since you can help them go places.

Still, your driving will become more and more of an issue as you age.

It is difficult to recognize that your driving skills are deteriorating, and you need help assessing them.

You'll be given all kinds of advice by friends and family, but it's wise to use the opinion of trained professionals instead.

Probably you should schedule a road test with a good driver-educator the first time someone suggests that you should think about giving up your license.

Thereafter, you should have another test every two years, or earlier if some event occurs which might affect your driving ability.

Surrendering the keys is an extremely emotional moment, and it's easy to quarrel with family members who are pressuring you.

Remember—they are showing that they care about you, your safety, and your peace of mind, so try not to be defensive or resentful.

Not Driving

Once you do give up driving, you may be subject to depression, and possible withdrawal from social contacts—it's essential to search strenuously for activities which will reinforce your feeling of self-worth and self-reliance.

You'll feel less independent, and less able to get places you used to go to. Still, there are a lot of things you can do.

If you live in a retirement residence, there will be regularly scheduled van trips for grocery and other shopping, for going to restaurants and entertainment, for sight-seeing excursions, and for being taken to doctor's and other appointments. It's not true independence, but it's not to be sneezed at, either.

There's public transportation, often including special buses available on call to take people wherever they need to go, and return them, as well—at a cost well below taxis.

Of course, there are taxis as well—expensive, sure, but it's nice to know they're available for emergencies.

As for going places in other people's cars, don't put too much reliance on this—unless someone is willing to commit to a regular date, every week or every month, or for some specific regular purpose. Other people's schedules are so full and so subject to change, that there's usually not much you can count on.

There's one alternative I'm trying to use, now that I'm not driving. I've kept my car, and asked the counselor of a nearby high school to find a student I can hire (this could also be done at a local college) to drive me in my own car a few times a week to wherever I want to go. It hasn't worked yet, but I'm still trying.

"Not driving" is not the end of the world, although it may seem like it at the time. Rather, it's a challenge to see how creatively you can deal with one more problem.

CHAPTER 20

Pills, Pills, Pills, Pills, Pills

The Medication Morass

The title says it all. Sooner or later every retired person is going to feel swamped by pills. I counted recently, and found I was taking 16 a day. Just remembering is a chore. Making sure nothing is omitted or repeated is a challenge.

When I grew up in the 1920's and '30's, pills were dispensed only in the event of illness. They were sometime things, and disappeared once one felt better. There was very little round-the-calendar medication, and not much of the over-the-counter array we see in stores today.

But, with the population living longer, and chronic ailments coming into the picture, prescriptive medications to control them have become standard. In addition, food supplements and alternative medicines have caused an explosion in the over-the-counter market.

The challenge of pills hits different people at different times. You may be able to defer it for a long period. But by a certain age, there doesn't seem to be anybody who's exempt. And the task becomes one of handling it efficiently and effectively, which isn't as easy as you might think. Then for some, in addition to pills, there may be inhalers, patches, and injections—even oxygen.

A standard problem is asking yourself, "Have I taken such and such today." You do remember taking it, or them. But was it today, or yesterday? You don't want to skip, and your doctor doesn't want you to skip, but both of you specially don't want you to take anything twice.

To be totally consistent requires a system, and absolute regularity. But doing things like this doesn't come naturally to most of us. We tend to see this approach as compulsive and controlling, and we'd like to be a little more laid back. In the following list I give a few suggestions for gaining control over your pills. I hope they're helpful.

To be frank, this reliance on pills will last the rest of your days. Whether it becomes a matter of routine, or a mild annoyance, or a constant irritation, is up to you. But you must find a way to come to terms with it, so that any negative feelings you have don't become a drain on your energy and happiness, nor a motivation causing you to make mistakes. It's my opinion that if you achieve a repetitive pattern with which you're comfortable, it will be the best way to do this.

But now I feel the need to add a warning, especially if you're getting prescriptions from several sources. It's easy in such a case to take too many drugs, perhaps without anyone realizing it. This might do damage, including dangerous interactions, or even addiction. You should have a physician or pharmacist review your portfolio of medications, including all over-the-counter items you take regularly.

Good luck with your pill performance!

Pills, Pills, Pills, Pills, Pills

Sometimes, it seems as if the life of a senior revolves around pills. An increased number comes with the territory. As for me, I take them too, divided between prescriptive meds and food supplements.

Organizing and managing a large number is difficult—it's hard to be certain we've taken every one, and each only once, unless a plan's in place for not forgetting or double-dosing.

Many persons use a compartmented pillbox, perhaps labeled for days of the week, although this method may not work if the number of pills is large—you might need two pillboxes.

Others rely on lists, or reminders by a housemate, or other memory devices, but no method seems to be foolproof. I myself sort my pills for the day soon after I get up, putting them in small dishes, according to the time they're to be taken—empty dishes give me reassurance.

Whatever you do, it's important not to forget or double-dose on any frequent basis. If you do, talk to your doctor, and get someone to help you devise a better system—missing an occasional dose won't do much damage, but taking two doses often could be harmful.

If you can't find some way to take your meds confidently and correctly, you'll have to arrange for someone to take charge, and dispense them to you as needed.

Prescription medications often develop into a major expense for many seniors. If this is a worry to you, you should know there are sources of help. There's a list on this subject in Chapter 4.

Splitting pills can sometimes save money, although the drug producers seem to be trying to stop this, and some medications are not capable of being split.

Drug Addiction

Perhaps I go too far afield with a topic like 'drug addiction,' since I certainly don't assume there are many users in an average group of retirees.

At the same time, there's always a risk when anyone is taking a large number of drugs on a regular basis.

In the preceding list, I give suggestions for keeping your pill-taking in order. Now, I want to say something about keeping it from becoming a danger.

A great many of the over-the-counter remedies or food supplements you take present little or no risk. Also, a large number of prescription drugs are not addictive, and are dangerous only in the event of an accidental overdose. Still, you may have some medicines, often pain relievers, which must be handled very carefully.

In addition to the procedures and precautions I've already listed, you should take extra care, especially with addictive drugs. First, ask your doctor or pharmacist which ones they are, so you can keep an eye on them. Then, store them apart from your other medications, so they can't be easily taken in error.

And when you do take them, make a record each time you do, to prevent accidental overdoses, and so that you know, and so does your doctor, how much you're using.

It's particularly important not to get in the habit of taking extra pills occasionally, because of pain. If you do, keep a record. It's easy to take too much without realizing it, once you begin using more and more to get relief—you can get hooked.

Don't become an accidental addict!

Chapter 21

Food and Beverage
Doing It Right!

The first issue in this category is cooking. For one thing, if the non-cooker or the seldom-cooker is the one who retires, there's a need to discuss changes in this responsibility, There are many retirees, usually women, who feel they've been cooking since forever, and they've earned the right to slack off or quit.

But eating remains a necessity, and preparing food has to be done. An early task of any new retiree to decide, with or without help, how to manage it. Eating out is pretty pricey, while continually serving pre-prepared food gets boring, and cooking a lot is the thing you're trying to change.

No one, certainly including me, can tell you what to do. It depends on your abilities and interests. All I can say is that you should make what you think are sensible plans, try them out, and adjust accordingly. You'll probably end up with some combination of eating out inexpensively, buying a wide variety of prepared foods, and doing some simple cooking.

You probably think cooking is something about which you need no advice—especially if you've been keeping house for a lifetime. This is certainly true while you're still in your active years, and particularly so if you're still in your own home. The only change which might take place then is different sharing of kitchen time.

But, if you face budget constraints, or move to smaller quarters, and especially if you enter a retirement residence, changes are called for. I try in my ensuing remarks to indicate some possibilities. You'll need to show a lot of ingenuity, and do much improvising, if you have to deal with limited storage space, or if your facilities make some kinds of cooking, like frying, unfeasible.

Also, you should think of any limitations your physical state might place on you. If your memory's slipping, you have to guard against leaving the stove on and forgetting it. Not only does this damage the utensil and possibly the stove, but it risks a fire and/or injury to the forgetter. It is to avoid such problems that assisted living quarters often contain no oven or stovetop—only a microwave.

Then, your ability to stand for a lengthy period of time (especially if you're on a cane or walker) may make cooking an enterprise which has to be simpler and more limited. Perhaps your interest in doing it, and your willingness to put in long hours in the kitchen, will dwindle. You may even find yourself disinterested in the tasks of food preparation— shopping, storing, cooking, cleaning up, and the rest.

In short, you need to invest yourself in the issues I've outlined, and re-think the matter from time to time, especially when there's a change in your living arrangements. You'll find that cooking becomes more of a concern than you expect it to be, and often a major one in the later years of your life. I make a few suggestions in the list which follows.

When I first planned this book, I didn't contemplate saying anything about eating and drinking. I felt there was so much material from dietitians, and so much information about the dangers of drinking, that there was little of value I could say. Many people are willing to give information and advice about your diet, especially if you're trying to lose weight, or at least, not gain it. Likewise, warnings about the risks of alcohol abound everywhere.

I've changed my mind, obviously, and it will be up to you to decide whether I was wrong to do so. I changed it because I felt that even though I couldn't advise you about the food pyramid or Alcoholics Anonymous, I could at least suggest some ways in which you might come to terms with them, and similar matters.

Proper eating is so important in older people that I must make some suggestions on how to deal with food consumption. Paying attention to this can well lengthen your life span, while neglect and improper habits can certainly shorten it. The advice I give in the list which follows represents ways I've dealt with my own food practices.

In addition, if I don't say something about drinking, I neglect one of the world's most commonly enjoyed pleasures. Of course, there are many for whom alcohol is anathema, and for some, tantamount to sin. I hope I don't offend any of them with what I have to say. I respect both them and their position, and since my mother and grandmother were in their day both officials in the Women's Christian Temperance Union, I'm certainly well acquainted with the viewpoint.

Still, there are millions of people, including retirees, who drink responsibly, and find it relaxing, and a socially useful practice. It is for them that I make my remarks, which again represent what I've learned from my own life experiences.

Cooking

As has already been suggested, kitchen responsibilities need to be re-thought when either (or both) of a couple retires.

For many people, the cooking chores of a lifetime begin to wear down in the later years of life.

A weariness with kitchen work often comes at a time when eating in restaurants presents a financial burden.

The older you get, the more you'll look for ways to simplify your cooking procedures.

Finding a middle ground requires sharing the load, using food which requires heating rather than cooking, and evaluating all food purchases in terms of their ease of preparation.

Converting to a continental breakfast, or a soup-and-sandwich (or -salad) lunch or supper, or both, can lower the workload.

Some people switch to a two-meals-a-day schedule.

Another practice is to schedule one day a month when you prepare meals for several days—to be frozen, and re-heated later.

Many older couples take their main meal in the middle of the day at a family restaurant, taking advantage of lower lunchtime prices, and possibly taking home leftovers for supper.

One major reason for considering a retirement residence is the availability of its dining room.

Eating

As at all ages, we need to watch our eating habits. It's even more important after 65, since bad habits have greater effect.

All dietitians recommend three balanced meals a day, while the lack of a morning rush in retirement makes a <u>good</u> breakfast possible.

A balanced meal means at least protein, starch, and vegetable or fruit. Don't drift into a continental breakfast because it's easy.

Not hungry for breakfast? Take a short walk.

Beside meat and eggs, breakfast protein can also be cheese or peanut butter.

Eggs are probably not eaten enough. There are so many ways to serve them—fried, scrambled, poached, shirred, omelets, soft-boiled, hard-boiled. Three times a week is not too much.

Grabbing food hastily should be abandoned—quick food almost always is highly caloric and usually not well balanced.

Eating at varying times, or in front of the TV makes for less-balanced meals. Also, it's hard to keep track of your intake.

Some nourishing foods which are little used include cream of wheat, muesli, rice, rye bread, nuts, applesauce, tofu.

It's commonly reported that two cups of coffee a day is healthy. Tea is particularly good for you, most notably, green tea.

Don't allow your food intake to decline, especially if you're losing weight. Talk to your doctor.

If nothing tastes good, or you have no appetite, try using spices.

Don't eat alone.

Drinking

If you're a non-drinker, don't take anything I say as a suggestion that you start.

Research shows that moderate drinking, certainly no more than two a day, is healthful, especially red wine.

A higher level of alcoholic intake than this may shorten your life, and the higher the level the greater the damage.

If you have any doubt at all about any drinking you do, get your doctor's advice.

Table wine has been considered an essential part of meals for centuries.

All alcoholic beverages are caloric, and many have little food value, so be careful if you're trying not to gain weight.

A shot of whisky (1 1/2 ounces), a 12-ounce can of beer, and a 5-ounce glass of table wine all have about the same amount of alcohol.

Short drinks, like cocktails and liqueurs, are often consumed at a fast rate, so they may add more calories and more risk.

Alcohol slows your responses, making driving particularly unwise for an older driver, whose response time has already slowed.

Drinking is best when it's a social activity—a little goes a long way to stimulate social interaction.

Don't drink alone.

CHAPTER 22

Recreation

Live It Up a Little!

The vision of the golden years, so lovingly depicted in advertisements for retirement communities, cruise lines, and other dream-boat activities, is an illusion. I've already stated that those who try to live this way find they soon look for more meaningful things to do.

Nonetheless, recreation is a vital part of life, and increasingly so as one ages, although its nature may change. Extreme physical activities become less feasible. And many things which occupied you before retirement have disappeared, leaving you with blocks of time to fill meaningfully. What do you do?

On the next page, I list some recreations which will be available to you throughout the rest of your life. Many are extensions of what you've always done. But some are calculated to be of interest as you age. The list is by no means complete, and you should use it to stimulate thought of other possibilities.

Many of my suggestions make no demands on your physical capabilities. There are board games, bingo, puzzles, and similar mental challenges. There are quiet outdoor activities like croquet and putt-putt golf, and of course there are the old standbys—TV, movies, music, and reading. In addition, there are computer and video games for people interested in electronic devices.

Almost everything pleasant can be made into a recreational recourse—walking, hiking, ping pong, pool, book clubs, discussion groups, classes, dancing, movies, theater-going, you name it. The list is endless, and determined by what you enjoy, what costs are involved, what is possible under existing conditions, and whether needed companions are available. The recreations you choose will differ for every one, and each of you must plan your own. Fortunately, this is both easy and fun.

It's sad to see someone without possibilities—a person who never seems to have anything enjoyable to do, who says, "I'm bored." Such an individual, whether she knows it or not, is simply waiting for the inevitable to happen. And this is likely to come sooner rather than later, certainly sooner than for her fellow retirees who are living more fulfilled lives.

So I say, do not fail to make recreation a part of your life—especially with an eye to what can continue into later years. It matters little what form it takes, although many activities have additional values. Any form of recreation has a restorative value. It keeps you active (I've already discussed this at some length). It makes you feel younger. It usually gives you a chance to socialize (Another value I've discussed), and it gives you something to look forward to (ditto).

So hop to it. Plan a life in which recreation gets a chance to do what its name suggests—a re-creation of you and your well-being.

Recreational Activities

Many outdoor physical activities, like golf or croquet or hiking, can be enjoyed even though your capabilities decline.

Just plain walking can be made into a regular pleasure, as the weather permits—and when it doesn't, indoor walking is usually possible in a shopping mall.

Dancing, or just listening to music you enjoy, is good fun, and the former also provides physical activity.

If you can still access an outdoor area, gardening is an option.

Card games are often a resource for older people, especially gin rummy (or canasta), pinochle, poker, and bridge—the king of card games (in my opinion).

There are many other card games—cribbage, hearts, single or double solitaire, euchre, casino, etc.—that you might like to learn, if you don't know them already.

Then, there are board games—backgammon, chess, checkers, Monopoly, Clue, Parcheesi, Othello, Chinese checkers, Pictionary, etc. You might like to find what's available, and see what interests you.

Trivial Pursuit is particularly enjoyed by older people, especially when the questions deal with the past.

All I can say about Bingo is to note that many people really enjoy it and its socializing. It too can be continued into advanced old age.

I also don't comment on gambling. Often, it's available only after long trips, and it risks costing more money than many can afford. Yet, it offers recreational values to many people.

What about jigsaw puzzles? For those who like them, they provide hours of pleasure, especially working jointly with others.

Going Out

All through life, 'going out' is a symbol of recreation. As a young person, it's part of your growing independence—of being able to do on your own what you choose to do. Later, it's a symbol that you're not just tied down to job, or family, or household.

In retirement, it remains a symbol—that you're still able to get around, even at night, that you're still able to enjoy recreation where it's to be found, and that you're still in control of a major part of life.

In the early retirement years, going out, especially in the evening, is much the same as it has been for most of your life—without the hassle of arranging for baby-sitting.

As time wears on, however, you tend to feel tired in the evening, and loath to expend the energy (and perhaps. the money). It seems simpler and more comfortable to stay home, watch the TV, read, do puzzles, chat with friends, or just be comfortable.

Too much of this should be resisted. If you have an active interest, like the theater, the movies, concerts, dancing, eating out, visiting friends or family, you should make a real effort to continue—hopefully, at least once a week.

Staying home too much tends to lower your energy level, put you in a rut, and narrow your interests. If going out has been a major part of your life in the past, it should still be part of your life as long as you're physically able to get out of the house.

If you can't drive at night, arrange for a joint expedition with friends or family members—or even take a taxi. You don't have to make the excursion elaborate—just going to the movies or a restaurant will do. The act of doing it has a revivifying effect.

If you do get into the habit of going out, you'll find that it occupies your attention and thoughts beyond the moment itself, and serves to keep you alert.

CHAPTER 23

Traveling

The Great Indulgence

Traveling is a difficult topic to handle, perhaps because it means so many things to so many people. It can range all the way from an overnight visit to Aunt Ellie in the next county to a cruise around the world. And of course the expense varies no less wildly.

A lot of what I have to say on this subject might change if I knew something about your finances. It would also depend on your interest in other countries, your tolerance of long car trips, or long flights, or ocean voyages, your prior travel experiences, and your available time and health.

I'll start by confessing my own experiences. I've been an inveterate traveler all my life, starting at 9 years of age, when my parents took me on a four-month journey to Palestine and Europe. Later, my visits to other parts have included lengthy stays in England, France, Canada, Japan, the Philippines, and many parts of the U.S. I've also made many shorter trips to other countries. Finally, I've cruised a lot (something over 25), including recent ones to the Mediterranean and the Pacific coast of Mexico. After all, think about how many opportunities 94 years have afforded me.

So, you need to realize that I'm a fan of traveling, and judge my remarks accordingly. I've always found the experience revivifying, and always returned home dead-tired and exhilarated. For devotees, there's simply nothing like it, and we justify the expense by noting how much longer our memories last than that new car or TV, or those other luxuries.

However, I have many friends whose greatest pleasure is returning to the same spot to vacation—year after year after year. They find great comfort in renewing moments which they've already enjoyed so much. And I also have friends who prefer to stay home. They say, and I know they mean every word of it, that there's no place in the world they'd rather be, and they look forward to a vacation, or other special time, when they can do things to or for their home, and cherish relaxing and luxuriating in it.

For such people, much of what I have to say here is useless. Further, their obvious pleasure in the patterns they' choose leads me to believe that for them, their choices are just right. But, there are also many people who hear the same call that I do, and it is for them that I make a few further remarks.

The first has to do with money. Much foreign travel has become almost ridiculously expensive, especially the popular destinations of Great Britain and Europe. Many other locations are relatively cheaper, although still high. But a lot of these are in third-world countries, or other less-developed areas, where the health delivery system may not be up to American standards.

So, since I'm assuming that you're watching your money, I'm also assuming that many foreign destinations are out of the question, at least for the time being. If this isn't true for you, and you're well enough heeled to challenge the foreign exchange rates, t envy you, and you may not need my cost-saving hints.

I think, however, that most retirees are much like me, with enough to last us, but only if we exert a little care. We find that going abroad is perhaps feasible if we can pay for it in American dollars. This means pre-paying most or all of our anticipated expenses before leaving home. Often, this involves joining a group tour, where the travelers are transported together, sightsee together, eat together, and stay in the same hotels.

I'll not say a lot about tours, since they vary widely. They come in all price levels, vary greatly in the size of the group and the crowding in any coaches used, and in the amenities provided. The price depends on such factors, as well as the quality of the meals and rooms provided, the length of the tour and the distance traveled, and whether or not the travel is off-season. Because of the variety of offerings, and the presence of some doubtful operators, you should use a travel agent of good reputation for booking anything. Remember—if the advertisement makes a trip sound too good to be true, it probably is!

Since I have mostly traveled independently, I have had only limited contact with a tour group—on only half a dozen occasions. So I shall not add much on the subject. I will say, though, that you should be very concerned about the number of seats in a coach compared to the number of persons to occupy them—especially if the trip is long or the weather rainy. Not being able to move around is a real inconvenience. So is the inability to be in the right location to take a picture of something which passes quickly.

Another point to remember is that you often are subject to one-night stays in hotels, which mean you live out of a suitcase. If leaving, you have to leave your packed bags outside your room before you go to breakfast. Also, laundry can be a problem.

In spite of all the negative comments I've made, though, group travel is the only feasible way for many, particularly women alone, to go where they want to. I have known many such, as well as married couples, who do it over and over, with great satisfaction.

Some people seek to save money by booking an inexpensive tour and using only the transportation, rooms, and meals it offers. They feel these three features are offered less expensively that they could obtain by themselves, and with less effort. Possibly, this is true, but it requires a lot of sophistication on the part of the traveler, as well as the ability to manage one's own sightseeing. I make this suggestion for those who would like to try it. I don't recommend it generally.

A major way of managing the costs of travel is by cruising, where your food, room, and transportation are all paid for in advance, and you know what your trip will cost. (There are some warnings on this latter point, however, which I consider below and in the lists to follow.)

Cruise travel has become more and more popular in recent years. This has led companies to build bigger and bigger ships, in order to decrease the cost per traveler. There has also been more and greater competition, with the result that prices have kept to a fairly reasonable level.

What the companies have done to offset fares affected by competition is to provide all kinds of add-ons at extra cost. They charge for beverages, photographs, shore trips, spa, specialty restaurants. They have a casino and stores on board. You can get away from much of this, though. You don't have to drink, or use the spa, or the restaurants. You don't have to shop or gamble. And you can do shore trips on your own, with or without guides and drivers, either without cost, or at a much lower one.

Another additional expense for the passenger is the amount given as tips, which you really can't get away from. You can decide on how much to give, and who you'll give it to, and to that extent it's under your control. But tipping is such a part of the experience that you can't just forgo it, any more than you can in a restaurant at home. Meanwhile, the cruise lines are encouraging you to let them do it for you automatically, and/or suggesting how much should be given.

Then, there's the cost of getting to the port of embarkation and back, together with any expenses there. (Sometimes, the transportation cost will be included in the price quoted by the cruise line, but don't count on it.) The result of all this is that you have to look at these items to determine how much a cruise is going to cost. I usually expect them to add at least 25 percent to the basic cruise price. Your experience may be higher or lower.

I've spent a lot of time on the costs of travel. But there are other considerations as well, including your health. There's the question of whether you can get good medical attention you might need away from home, as well as the issue of whether your physical condition is good enough to withstand the rigors of travel. You can get advance information on both these points, the first on the internet, e.g., on the website of the Centers for Disease Control, the second from your doctor. One advantage of cruising is that there's a doctor and medical facilities on board.

If there is any doubt in your mind about the possibility of your needing medical assistance abroad, take out special insurance to cover it—as well as medical evacuation, if needed. Actually, I think insurance is always a good idea, even for you who are in the best of health, since there are so many ways a trip can be interrupted, or even canceled, by unexpected events. Frequently advance payments are not refundable, or otherwise lost.

I'll add little more about travel. There's the question of sailing on cargo ships, or windjammers. There's the area of highly specialized trips built around special interests or abilities, like ecological excursions, adventurous travel, and outdoor activities for those physically highly fit. But these are of interest only to a minority. In addition, I know very little about them.

Travel is so much a matter of your specific interests. Once you've dealt with the problems of finances and health, you're pretty much on your own. I'll add only that as your strength and stamina decline, your choices narrow. Still, you can do cruising into advanced old age.

Traveling

Many retirees look forward to doing lots of traveling. Frequently, it doesn't work out that way.

One reason, of course, is cost. If it's foreign travel you wish, the falling value of the dollar has really hurt the American traveler.

Domestic travel is another matter, and many retirees spend considerable time, especially during their first few years, going to places they've always wanted to see, or visiting friends or family in distant locations.

Travel can put a big hole in the budget, and with health costs increasing as you age, and perhaps a concern about how long your money will last, you may well want to spend it other ways.

Possibly, as you recall the many memorable trips you've had, there may be fewer and fewer places you're dying to see.

Health has a major influence on travel. There's a concern about needing care or treatment away from home—especially in a foreign country with a poor-quality health-delivery system. Even in the U.S., you may not want to rely on strange health providers, and if you have recurrent health problems, you may tend to stay home.

In most foreign countries, Medicare does not provide coverage, so health care abroad can be expensive. You should buy special insurance—another cost factor. Actually, you should insure the entire trip since many advance payments can be lost.

Finally, if you have trouble getting around, or have vision or hearing problems, the pleasure of travel diminishes, and the energy called for may become burdensome.

As for me, I'll travel as long as I can set one foot in front of the other, and have two pennies to rub together. I find travel exhilarating and revitalizing, and if you're like me, you do, too. Keep doing it as long as you can!

Escorted Tours

For the older traveler, who doesn't want the hassles of finding his own hotels and transportation, and deciding for himself what he wants to see, the escorted tour is an easy solution.

In some ways, escorted tours are like cruises—only on land. Included are transportation (usually in the same coach for the duration), meals (usually breakfast and dinner only), and accommodations in hotels arranged by the tour operator.

With a guide to tell you what you're seeing and answer questions, and a group of fellow-travelers who quickly become friends, you're set for an easy and pleasant way to sightsee.

Of course it's more expensive than going by yourself, although sometimes not so much as you think—there are a number of companies who specialize in modest costs. Still, you're paying for the time and expenses of the guide, and for the costs and profit of the organization setting up the tour.

There are certain disadvantages. One is that you're often limited to one suitcase. Another is that you have to be packed and ready to go each travel day, with your bag outside your hotel room, before you go to breakfast. A third is that there's rarely an opportunity to linger at a spot you enjoy—the coach has to leave. Finally, you have to be careful that the tour has not sold too many seats—any extended tour should have no more than half the seats taken. This of courses adds to the cost.

The escorted tour is a particular blessing to anyone who needs to travel alone—there's companionship at all times, and the tour operator can arrange for you to have a roommate or not as you wish (single occupancy is an extra charge).

Tours are available for every location, here and abroad, for almost any time of the year, for different-sized groups, and at almost every price-level from basic to luxury.

Cruises

Cruises might well have been specially invented for the retiree—they go all year round, accommodate every size group, have activities for all ages, sightseeing for the infirm or disabled, foreign travel without packing and unpacking, and all at a fixed price known in advance. What more can you ask for?

For the aging traveler, it's almost ideal—less energy required, no need to do anything one is not up to at the moment, and a chance to see exotic places in comfort, and with a doctor at hand.

It's not quite so simple as the cruise lines make it sound, though. To start, the all-inclusive fare is not that—in addition to things like port taxes or fuel supplements, which are disclosed in the brochure, you pay for beverages on board, you may pay extra for eating in special dining rooms, you pay if you use the spa, and you pay for any shore trips you take. And as you night expect, everything supplementary is charged at high rates.

Then there is tipping, which is no more optional than at a restaurant at home. It's usually added to your bill, unless you opt out, and will be about ten percent of your basic cruise price.

In addition, you frequently have to pay extra to fly to the port of embarkation (which might be abroad), and if the cruise line books your air, the charge is usually higher than if you book yourself. However, if you do the latter you should arrive a day early, since the ship will not wait for a late arrival.

You should buy your cruise from a good specialist, because prices vary widely, as does the age of the average traveler on each line. You need help avoiding noisy cabins, those with poor sight-lines, and those remote from the dining room. Also be sure to get trip insurance—cruise fares are not refundable.

All in all, cruises are a relaxing, comfortable, pleasant way to go, especially for older people. I think them well worth the money. Occasional re-routings or delays don't spoil the pleasure.

Tips for Cruises

Obviously, I recommend cruising—I've done it myself—many times, starting in 1958. I'll add a few points I've found helpful.

You can avoid the expense of shore trips by planning to go on your own—bring a good guide-book, and arrange with another couple to hire a car and driver jointly. Read the guide-book in advance, decide what you want to see, and then tell the driver. You'll be able to see everything you want at half the price. You'll also avoid the crowding and the on- and off-ing of tour buses, and by leaving a little later in the morning you can choose a taxi without being besieged.

Eating in a special dining room may be exciting, but you're paying for a meal when an excellent one is awaiting you at your normal table without extra charge. Eating ashore can be expensive, although often a welcome change. You can plan your time on land in such a way as to have lunch or a snack on board. Also, buying snacks and bringing them back to the ship avoids the expensive cost of similar items offered in the cabin display or the ship's store.

Beverages are very much an individual choice. All drinks are costly on a cruise ship, and you're not allowed to bring your own alcoholic beverages on board. Presumably, anything you drink in your cabin is provided (and charged for) by the ship. Free drinks may be available at one of more parties hosted by the cruise line. Otherwise, you're on your own.

Other expenses, like the spa, the casino, the ship's shopping area, the art auctions, the photographs taken of you, can just be ignored, unless they appeal—I've found that indulging in them adds up quickly.

Still, so much is included: all kinds of activities, dance and other classes, informative talks, movies in your cabin, briefings on each port, stage shows every evening, opportunities to make new friends, that I find a cruise very rewarding.

CHAPTER 24

Pets

Comfort and Companionship

What to say about pets?

You may feel very strongly about the matter—pro or con. You may be a cat lover or a dog person, or be attached to some other creature—bird, or fish, or whatever.

Nothing I say will change any of this. And yet, I do feel the need to discuss the question.

I've seen newspaper reports that people with pets tend to live longer than those without. I'm not sure why this is so, unless it has something to do with a lowered level of stress, and a calming effect on your peace of mind. It can be heartwarming to think that a creature you care about reciprocates the feeling.

Or perhaps, the self-discipline involved in tending to a pet's needs on a daily basis, and knowing that you're essential to a creature which might not otherwise survive, can lead to a sense of confidence and self-worth.

Regardless, it's a fact that a pet can help you extend your life. So, no matter what decision you make on the issue, you make it in possession of this knowledge.

I'll finish with a confession. I'm one of the dog lovers, and I have mine living with me in an apartment, in spite of the fact that he has a tendency to bark and annoy the neighbors when left alone. This limits my social life to some extent, and my efforts to train him still have to prove their effectiveness.

Yet I gain so much satisfaction that I consider the positive considerations far outweigh the negative. In addition, since I have to tend to his outdoor needs, I feel he does a lot for my physical well-being.

In view of all this, you may want to evaluate my comments, based on my proclivities.

On the next page, I list a few suggestions for the use of those of you who are either pet lovers, or open to the possibility.

Pets

There doesn't seem to be much difference in the satisfaction different kinds of pets afford their owners, in spite of the pre-disposition of any pet-lover to consider that her choice is superior to that of others. I find many people get extraordinary pleasure from their pets.

Almost always, the time and money spent on a pet is greater than you anticipate—this is true for all pets, but some cost more than others. Dogs appear to be the most expensive, with the possible exception of exotic creatures—which I know nothing about.

Some of the expenditure is discretionary, such as the cost of pet-food, frequency of veterinary check-ups, and the amount of care you might pay for.

It's probably a good idea to have a pet which at least one other member of the family likes, since there may be times when you'll have to ask someone to look after the pet for a while.

It's also a good idea to think about what will happen in the event you become incapacitated or die. You need to have someone who has agreed to take care of the pet, or otherwise handle the matter to your satisfaction in such an event.

Pets can create a problem when you move or travel, and you need to plan for such times.

Some pets, like cats and dogs, have more potential for causing damage and being nuisances than others, especially those kept mainly in cages or tanks.

You may have a problem if you plan to move into an apartment or retirement residence, since most of these places have policies regarding pets, and some ban most or all of them.

CHAPTER 25

Sharing Quarters
Staying Close

For many retirees who are married couples, sharing quarters is a non-issue. If they've been married long enough to reach retirement age together, they've pretty well sorted out their problems. And if they marry close to, or after, retirement, they've done so out of a mature and experienced judgment.

Indeed, I seriously considered not saying anything at all on this subject. But then I got to thinking about widows and widowers who might seek a spouse or companion, and about single persons of both sexes, who might feel that sharing quarters could cure loneliness and help financially.

So here I go.

A lot I've already said about changes in relationships applies also to couples living in the same housing unit. Obviously, they need to make plans for sharing responsibilities, and for working together on homemaking tasks. They need to divide their living space in such a way that both parties are happy, and both have a satisfactory location for their own possessions. But, they confront additional challenges, especially if they come to a shared life after some time as singles.

For one thing, they must recognize that each has built a pattern of habits over the years, and the likelihood that these will merge seamlessly is very small. Both need to acknowledge this, and refrain from insisting on their own ways. This is often hard to do, since each is likely to apply his own way almost automatically, and without realizing it might crowd the other.

The situation requires open discussion, with both housemates reporting on their own habits, and each soliciting suggestions from the other. The more this can be done calmly and courteously, the better. In particular, both parties should refrain from speaking angrily on the spur of a moment of irritation, but should reserve comments for a later, calmer session.

It's probably a good idea, especially in the beginning stages of a relationship, to schedule regular times at which both persons can speak of their needs and concerns, and both can make an effort to see the other's point of view, and, if possible, accommodate it. The key is effective communication, without heat or criticism, so that each understands where the other is coming from. It's important not to comment negatively about any habits or practices of the other, although you can reveal how they make you feel.

Another potential issue is that of space—not physical space alone, but psychological space as well. Two people living together in quarters which may be confining, see and hear each other endlessly. This can easily become abrasive, unless steps are taken to avoid it. Both parties need time and space to be by themselves, and do things they don't have to share. Joint planning and honest discussion are needed to accommodate this need. It's essential.

Finally, I'd like to comment on the fact that two people rarely age at the same pace and in the same manner. Their capabilities may be close to equal when they start a relationship, only to diverge as one begins to fail, or develop special needs. Probably, this possibility should be discussed at the very beginning, with both parties considering how much assistance they can promise the other. Then, when a circumstance of need arises, both will know what to expect. But it's hard to anticipate all that might occur.

On the following page, I give a few suggestions I hope will be useful.

Sharing Quarters

Coordinating the separate habit patterns which two persons have solidified over many years is a monumental task—even more so if either (or both) has lived alone for any length of time.

This challenge must be addressed through open and honest communication, without nagging, criticism, or anger.

Both partners will need space—to be alone at times, to be left alone when either feels it's necessary, or to engage in independent activities. This freedom should be readily granted by the other party without complaint, ill-feeling, or self-pity.

It's essential that space allocations be acceptable to both parties. If either feels unfairly treated, the living arrangement will not work.

Needless to say, there must be equitable division of all household responsibilities, including finance. There should be a clear agreement about each person's obligations, and how and when they'll be performed. Perhaps a simple agreement might be put in writing.

There should be regular opportunities to discuss changes, concerns, questions, or feelings, in a calm and non-accusatorial manner.

Regular complaints, constant nagging, or angry criticisms will destroy the living arrangement—often pretty quickly.

If the parties can find things they like to do in common—such as listening to music, watching television or movies, doing crossword puzzles together, or playing card games—the activity will go a long way to ensure the success of their partnership.

In brief, the more things the two have in common, and the more each is able to adjust to the other's needs and foibles, the better they'll be at quarter-sharing.

Chapter 26

Care-Giving

Loving Service

When I discussed the sharing of quarters above, I noted that one, or both, of the partners might develop special needs or disabilities. In such a case, the original arrangement between them, which was predicated on an equitable sharing of tasks and responsibilities, may no longer be feasible.

At the very least, this situation calls for the two to discuss openly the new circumstances and the options they have. Changes in living arrangements might be as simple as exchanging chores, so that the physically abler person does more of the active work, and the other takes on more non-physical jobs.

Often, though, more than this is called for. Sometimes, the individual with declining capabilities requires assistance with her personal everyday needs—taking medications, bathing, dressing, using oxygen, and the like. So, not only is she no longer capable of meeting her former responsibilities, but a number of additional tasks have been added to the household. And they have to be handled somehow.

Unless this is dealt with by the infirm individual's moving into assisted-living, the new circumstances call for someone to accept the new responsibilities. This someone can be the home-sharer who's already there, or it can be one or more helpers who come in to assist—or both.

In brief, the shared-living arrangement has morphed into a care-giving one.

As one who lived a care-giving role for several years, I have some thoughts on the subject. One is that the partner who still retains full capabilities is inclined to volunteer to do too much, especially if she cares deeply for the other person. This occurs because it's easy to look at the work of a single day, and think it's not too difficult to handle. It's harder to see that this daily responsibility, repeated over and over for months or years on end, can become more and more stressful.

When there's a close relationship between the partners, it's both natural and appropriate for the abler person to do things for the other. But, as I have just said, it's dangerously easy to try to do too much. This is a formula for possibly damaging the health of the care-giver, or perhaps inducing a growing feeling of resentment.

So, at the moment of decision, it's crucial for both persons to consider how much responsibility the care-giver can realistically assume over the long haul. Only in this way can the relationship can be preserved at the level both partners desire.

The only practical decision may be to employ one or more helpers to come in. There's a large number of organizations which provide this kind of service. However, their charges are not inconsiderable. Nonetheless, the cost of having care provided in one's own home is much less than that of entering a nursing facility, and may well approximate the cost of going into an assisted-living unit.

There are two key questions. The first is whether of not the level of care provided at home is as high as it should be. The second is how the person being cared for feels about it all. Indeed, this latter point is crucial for many people.

The sense of being tended to lovingly in comfortable, familiar surroundings is impossible to duplicate in a professional institution. I have sometimes said that a nursing facility emphasizes first the health and safety of the patient, while his happiness comes second, while at home the reverse is true. This is not to say that the subordinate consideration is ignored in either place. But it <u>does</u> say where the primary emphasis is in both.

My experience has been that the sense of comfort, supportiveness, and TLC felt by the party being tended to at home is so much higher than it is in an institution, that it goes a long way to increase the effectiveness of the care being given. I heard one lady in a nursing home say at one time, "This is the worst thing I've ever done." I've also heard a number of nursing-home attendants say that they've seen many patients just give up and stop trying—resulting in a rapid decline and early demise.

By now, you're probably assuming that I'm a fan of taking care of a person at home as long as possible. This is true. I feel the psychological benefits more than compensate for any technical inferiority of the professional health care. Of course, one tries to compensate to the greatest extent possible by employing helpers who are both capable and caring.

I shall end this discussion by repeating how important it is for both persons to express their feelings and desires as honestly as possible when a care-giving decision must be made, and for both to examine the alternatives fully. Only in this way can a commitment be made by the care-giver that has a chance of success, and preservation of the relationship at the highest level possible.

I present a few ideas in the following list.

Care-Giving

If you become a care-giver, you must be certain the task is within your physical and emotional ability to maintain over a long period of time.

In a strong relationship, there's a real risk that the care-giver will try to do too much. She must seek help and, especially, arrange for regular breaks.

Both persons involved should research alternatives as carefully as possible, and solicit the help and counsel of friends and family members in making a decision. They should solicit input from concerned observers and visitors, to ask if the latter notice developments which require attention.

Providing care to an individual works best when done in the home, if professional standards can be maintained.

You probably will need professional help, at least on a part-time basis—make contact with a number of organizations which provide care in the home before choosing one. Besides looking at such matters as costs, qualifications, services offered, and references, be sure to talk with one or more persons who've received care from each organization in the recent past. Care-giving will change the lifestyle of persons sharing quarters—housekeeping procedures will be different, and, probably, so will the social activities of the parties.

It's especially important to ensure that the care-giver will have opportunities to get away from time to time—she should have discretionary time to do whatever she wants to, and must not sacrifice cherished activities to the acts of giving care, nor should she be asked to.

If done properly, care-giving can become a bonding experience for both parties, resulting in a closer relationship than ever.

PART 4
- *Later Days* -

Hang In There!

None of us looks forward to aging, although as the saying goes, "It's better than the alternative." However, any plan for retirement life requires that you think about the time when your powers decline, and you're forced to adjust.

The adjustments can be of many kinds, from the possibility that you'll have to live in more secure quarters, to a need for assistance in daily living, to facing mental or physical disabilities. This last part of the book considers physical and mental decline, assisted living, nursing facilities, and end-of-life circumstances.

I know it's not comfortable to contemplate such conditions. But it's necessary to do it. I assume you agree. I'll try not to be alarmist or gloomy, but rather try to deal realistically with realistic concerns.

This is the last part of this book. When you're finished with it, I hope you'll be well on your way to a happy 100 years of age!

CHAPTER 27

Declining Health
Keep Doing Things!

Although unpleasant, the prospect of declining health faces everyone. For some fortunate persons, the decline is mild—possibly, slight loss of hearing or sight or balance. For others, it can be more severe, entailing the use of canes or walkers or wheelchairs or oxygen, or some combination thereof.

One thing we all encounter is some loss of balance, usually caused by deterioration in the inner ear. This creeps up on you so gradually that you may not be the first to notice. I can recall a grandson several years ago asking why I was lurching, and it suddenly dawned on me that I was doing that, and hadn't realized it until he spoke.

Since I'm not qualified to offer medical opinions, I'll leave it to professionals to advise you on what to do about any disability you might have. What I propose to do, instead, is look at how you can react to your health problems—in short, how to live with decline and disability.

The first thing I suggest is that you not talk too much about your health. I've noticed, in almost any gathering of older people, that their physical complaints, the cost and effectiveness of medications, and their experiences with doctors, tend to dominate the conversation. Although I think most persons truly care about how their companions are doing, there's a distinct limit to how much detail they wish to hear. The epitome of this issue is the situation where someone casually asks an acquaintance, "How're you doing today?"—only to be told on and on and on, in vast detail.

If you talk about your physical problems a lot, it implies that you think about them a lot. And this in turn implies that they're a worry to you. Although it's natural to worry about conditions which threaten your well-being, it's well known that dwelling too much on them doesn't help. Rather, it increases their impact on your peace of mind, and leads to their having a greater effect on your life than they should.

What you should do, once you've taken any action necessitated by a physical condition and recommended by your doctor, is think about it as seldom as possible. Concentrate, rather, on people, concerns, and activities which interest you. If you can do this, your problems will have less impact.

If you're given exercises to do, or other procedures are recommended, make a real effort to follow through on them. Not only will this make you feel you're taking constructive action, but it will tend to keep you from thinking constantly about your condition, and feeling sorry for yourself. The activity should also improve your physical condition.

A corollary to this is not to use a physical limitation as an excuse for saying "No" to suggestions that you participate in a desirable activity. I see many inhabitants of the retirement residence where I reside who have learned this—persons with disabilities who show a great capacity to "make do"—engaging in a wide variety of activities in spite of devices they tote around. I find them to be cheerful and positive, and determined to do what they want to do, regardless of impediments.

I'm not suggesting that you attempt things which you're clearly unable to handle physically. But you should consider, at the onset of any disability, if it absolutely precludes doing something you enjoy. If you decide it doesn't, make a determination not to use your physical limitations as an excuse at any time. When you can't accept an invitation, it's not because you "don't feel up to it," but because you've "scheduled something else."

Like the people I describe, try to remain as interested and active as possible, regardless of any disability you may have.

I've added four lists of ideas below. The first two consider health decline and coping with illnesses and accidents. The final pair deal with the related problems of loss of balance and the possibility of falling. These latter are common experiences among retirees, but are quite manageable, and I suggest some things you can do.

Since I started writing this book, I've had reason to apply many of my suggestions to myself, as I suffered a stroke in November, 2009. This resulted in considerable loss of control in my right arm and leg, and some slurring of speech. The secret of longevity may consist more in the ability to recover from illness than in simply avoiding it, and I'm trying to bounce back.

Today, eleven months later, I've made some progress. I've advanced from a wheelchair to a walker to a cane, and walk exclusively with the latter, although somewhat unsteadily. I hope and plan to continue my improvement to where I can walk without assistance, and have been given assurance by my therapists that I will. I've regained my ability to write my signature, to type with both hands on my word processor, and to write in longhand—although slowly, and somewhat unevenly. Then, my friends tell me my speech has cleared—more than I feel it has.

What I've tried to do is apply the suggestions which I make to you. I've tried to do so diligently, and my conclusion is that they helped me. I hope they help you too.

Dealing with Health Decline

Your basic emphasis should be on not allowing your debility to control your life. Rather, you should change your habits and activities to the least extent possible.

Be as realistic as you can be about any difficulties you have. Recognize their inevitability, if such is the case, and try not to feel sorry for yourself.

Recognize, too, that, although there may be things you can't do, there are many, many more that you can.

Try not to talk too much about your health or problems. Instead, develop areas of conversation which you enjoy, and which you think others might enjoy too.

Although hearing devices, vision enhancers, walking aids, and oxygen tanks are obviously visible, be as matter of fact about them as possible—try to keep them from intruding on anyone's enjoyment.

Learn to use competently any devices you must have, so that you don't embarrass yourself and make others uncomfortable by fussing with them.

Be knowledgeable about the financial aspects of any equipment you need to use. Medicare might underwrite some costs, and certainly they represent deductions on your tax return.

Regardless of how uncomfortable and/or unhappy you are about devices you're forced to use, and about any limitations on your activities, be confident that you'll get used to them. You'll begin to see them as helps rather than burdens, and eventually they'll become as much a part of you as glasses or watches.

Illnesses and Accidents

It may be that one of the secrets of longevity is not the ability to avoid disease, but the ability to bounce back after you incur it.

You will undoubtedly suffer at some time from illnesses or accidents or both. Your health and longevity are very much dependent upon your reaction.

In a way, the two afflictions in the title differ, but so far as their effects are concerned, they are very similar. In both, you have a period of distress, followed by a (seemingly too long) period of convalescence.

It's most important that you get competent professional advice from some one in whom you have confidence, and that you follow his recommendations precisely.

It's easy to say that what you're expected to do is too hard, or that you're too tired or feel too ill to do it, or that you'll do it later. It's at this point that you face a moment of truth. If you persevere, you have a chance to prevail—if you don't, you have the probability of failure.

I have found that it helps to schedule a procedure at the same time every day I'm supposed to do it. In that way, I don't have the temptation to delay for just a little while longer—instead, I know what and when I'm supposed to perform, and it's crystal clear if I'm responding in the right way or not.

I know from personal experience how difficult it is to do this on a regular basis. But all I can say is, "If you want to get and stay well, you'll do it—Period!"

Balance

Loss of balance is not the end of the world—it can be lived with.

It usually results from changes in the inner ear, although there may be other causes, such as side effects of medication.

Because loss of balance comes on gradually, you may not be fully aware of it until you find yourself staggering a lot, or even falling.

It's important to have your doctor check you out if this happens to you. He may have suggestions.

One thing you can do is join a balance class. This will not improve your balance so much as it helps you deal with it. Classes are often available at senior centers and retirement residences.

One technique taught is to identify your center of gravity, and keep it over your feet. I visualize a weight on a string attached to my chin, and try to keep the weight between my feet.

An exercise which is often used is to sit in a chair, plant your feet three to six inches apart on a pillow, and stand up several times in succession without pushing, or swinging your arms.

Another is to stand on the pillow, facing a mirror, close your eyes, and hold the pose for five seconds without twisting or dipping a shoulder (the mirror is to see how much contorting you do). This should be repeated several times.

Your physician may prescribe treatment by a physical therapist for your lack of balance. If so, you'll get a uniquely-designed, one-on-one program intended to maximize your chances of improvement. Such a program may require several months.

There is also WiiFit, for the Wii console, to test your balance, and give you challenges to help improve it, like skiing a course, rafting a river, or sinking balls in a hole, merely by shifting your weight on a balance board.

Falling

Falling is probably the accident most dreaded by an aging person. It often results in a broken hip, which takes a very long time to heal, if indeed it does at all.

So, the first thing to learn is how not to fall. The second is to learn how to fall, if indeed that should occur, in such a way as to minimize the chance of injury.

It's essential to maintain or improve your balance, as discussed in the previous list—loss of balance is a natural part of the aging process, and the most frequent cause of falls.

But, even without specialized help to improve your balance, there are a number of things you can do.

Remove things in your home which you might trip on or stumble over, like throw rugs, or badly placed small pieces of furniture.

Put grab bars in the bathroom and shower or bathtub, or indeed, anywhere there's a slippery surface.

While walking around the house, get into the habit of noting spots where you can take hold, or brace yourself, if needed.

Walking outdoors should be more of a conscious action than it has been in the past—note curbs and steps and uneven spots, and be careful where and how you put your foot.

Avoid walking on slippery surfaces. If it's necessary to do so, be sure to keep your weight forward, and put the fore part of your foot down before the heel, so that any fall is forward, not back.

If you do fall, try not to put a hand on the ground (which might cause a broken arm or shoulder), and try to fall as loose as possible (rigidity fosters broken bones).

Chapter 28

Assisted Living and Nursing Facilities
Keep Doing What You Can!

When you're still at home, or in what's called an independent-living unit, it's presumed you can manage your own life. However, there may come a time when it's hard to do what was previously easy. This can increase to a point where you're no longer able to cope, especially if you're single. Even with a housemate to help, it can get beyond you.

I refer to the basic functions of life—dressing, bathing, grooming, eating, taking medicine, or using bathroom facilities. If you can't handle all of these by yourself, and they've become too difficult for a care-giver to manage, or too constant for visiting professionals to provide, you need to think about the alternatives in the chapter title. They provide help in all the areas listed, and differ largely in how much care they provide, and how it's delivered.

Assisted living is a term used to describe apartments with pre-arranged care services provided on a scheduled basis. They're frequently located in a special area within a retirement residence (or they may be the sole type of unit in one). The retiree lives in an apartment similar to those for independent living, except that hazards like a cookstove have been removed, and there are personnel on the premises for her needs. A more recent development in some institutions is to scatter assisted living units among independent-living ones. In this way independent residents can obtain needed personal care on an ever-increasing basis without having to move to new quarters.

It's hard to know when someone's condition has passed beyond the possibility of remaining at home. It varies with the individual. Some people accept reality earlier, some struggle longer. Everyone involved with her tends to defer the decision as long as possible.

But, if you need help, you need help. If a problem exists with any of the functions listed above, that's a sign. So is too much forgetfulness, on the part of either the patient or caregiver. If this becomes chronic, especially regarding medications, it can do harm. And then, you face a decision.

Going into an assisted-living unit is often the next step. If you're already living independently in a residence, a move may be relatively easy—or not necessary if you're in a place which scatters assisted living throughout the building. But if you have to go to a new place, you have the task of choosing one carefully.

Doing this is quite similar to picking a retirement residence, which has already been discussed. You certainly need to visit, or have someone you trust visit. You need to get answers to your questions from people living there, and you (or a helper) need to go to the internet to see if there are complaints or other difficulties reported.

Remember that you're choosing what may be your life for many of its remaining years, and it's critical that you're some place where you feel safe, and happy, and well cared for. Choose wisely.

Life in an assisted-living unit, though, is often a way-station between being independent and entering a nursing home. To some extent, you're still independent, while concurrently receiving regular professional care. Between the scheduled visits of your helpers, however, you're left alone, or with your housemate. During such times, you're on your own, and if you can handle this, assisted living is for you. If you can't, you need a nursing facility.

Some people, especially if they're alone, find the intervals between visits of helpers to be difficult. If you have trouble with simple life tasks, you may also need help with the TV or other equipment, or have difficulty reading, or getting to the public rooms of the building. You have to decide what you're capable of, and choose accordingly.

Going to a nursing home may well be the final move of your life, and because of this, many persons find the prospect discouraging, or worse. Often, an older person will extract promises from her family not to be placed in one. And yet, if you have severe health needs, there's no reasonable alternative. Frequently, these needs can't be met at home, even with the procurement of a hospital bed and special equipment, plus the use of in-home professional helpers.

It may be that by the time you need a nursing home, you may have difficulty making decisions. It's possible that physical decline is accompanied by mental difficulties. In this case, the comments I've made are directed to those making decisions with you or for you.

In the ensuing lists, I look at choosing assisted living or a nursing facility, as well as how you, or your family, can deal with your residence in one or the other.

Choosing Assisted Living

When one or more of the basic tasks of personal care—dressing, bathing, grooming, eating, taking medicine, using bathroom facilities—are beyond your capabilities, it's time for assistance, either in your own home, or in a special unit.

In-home care is available from a number of organizations. If you employ one, they contract with you to provide an agreed-on number of visits a week on a scheduled basis, with agreed-on services, at an agreed-on price.

With a good organization, you'll have reasonable assurance of the capabilities and dependability of the helper who comes to the home, as well as professional supervision of her performance.

You need to choose the organization carefully, interviewing several, and talking with persons who have recently used the services of any you're serious about.

There's a distinct limit to how much care a housemate can or should assume. If the housemate is aging too, taking on too much might well lead to one more person needing special assistance.

You might prefer to move to an assisted living unit, with or without a partner, instead of having care-givers come to your home. These units are planned in such a way that helpers are available on the premise—they come at regularly-scheduled times to assist with specified tasks.

Choosing an assisted-living facility calls for all the steps recommended for selecting a retirement residence, as was discussed earlier. If the unit is in the same structure as your present dwelling, it makes the choice simpler.

Assisted Living

Life in an assisted-living unit has the disadvantage that, unless you have a housemate, you can be lonely and unsure of yourself between visits of helpers—since you may not be able to manage TV or other equipment, or get around the building.

Many assisted-living apartments have minuscule living rooms, to encourage residents to get out, use the public rooms, and have more interaction with others people.

Food is especially a problem, since few units have stove-tops or regular ovens, and some don't even have microwaves. Of course, three meals a day are normally provided. This can mean that help in getting to a dining room, or even in eating, may have to be part of the arranged schedule of assistance.

Of course, one of the advantages is that people are looking in on you regularly, and in the case of an emergency, someone will be with you quickly, even if you're unable to summon help.

Obviously, you'll not be in assisted living unless you've had considerable health decline, and I assume, therefore, that at least one family member will be checking on your welfare.

To this individual, I say that you should make observations and ask questions, as you would do in a nursing home.

You should observe the resident's interaction with helpers and be responsive to her complaints or dissatisfactions. You should note the physical condition of the unit, and ask whatever questions you feel are appropriate. Don't restrain yourself if anything at all seems to be wrong or amiss.

A high quality of life in assisted living is hard to maintain, since the resident often has many limitations. You have to be particularly creative in planning activities which are comparable to those of some one in independent living.

Choosing a Nursing Facility

A nursing facility may be the last home you'll occupy, so it should be chosen with particular care.

Since you'll get out seldom, or not at all, the environment must be a pleasant one to spend your time in.

The procedures and criteria for choosing a nursing facility are similar to those for an independent- or assisted-living residence, except that additional attention needs to be paid to the quality of the professional care, and the nurturing nature of the personnel.

It's important to make one or more unscheduled visits, to see how the personnel perform when they're not expecting you.

You should observe patients to note their alertness, cheerfulness, and general appearance of physical well-being. If some are able to answer questions, try to find out how they feel about the facility, and what they like and dislike.

You need to find out what medical services are available, and who provides them. If possible, you should try to talk with other patients who have used the same personnel. As a general rule, you will not be seeing your own physician, once you've entered a nursing facility.

You should check state listings, to see how the facility is rated, and what kinds and amounts of complaints have been recorded against it.

If possible, talk with persons visiting their own family members, to see what experiences they've had, and how they feel about the quality of care provided.

Dealing with a Nursing Facility

If you're in a nursing home, there will be many things you can't do for yourself, so there has to be at least one friend or family member checking on you regularly. I now speak to her.

It's important to personalize at least a portion of the room, with familiar things like pictures, bric-a-brac, a comfortable chair from home, etc.—this obviously will have to be done by some one else for the resident.

If she's declined mentally, I advise whomever is doing the checking to provide music, TV, or DVD—to the extent the patient is capable of enjoying them. If she can read, great! Give her as much as she wants. If she can't, read to her—especially what she enjoyed in the past. It can still be enjoyed even without full understanding. Furthermore, it's a form of bonding.

A good idea is to make a wall card in large print, giving the patient's name, age, working history, special interests, needs, etc. for the use of the varying personnel who'll be working with her, and for the benefit of visitors.

Most people in a nursing home share a room with another patient, so much of what I've said about sharing quarters will apply, if both patients are ambulatory and fairly active.

It's important that medications be carefully monitored. The nursing home has this responsibility, but its personnel should be observed from time to time, and questions asked to verity the accuracy of the list, and the amount and frequency of doses, since there's much turn-over of nurses and aides.

Members of the family should visit often, particularly noting changes in the physical condition or attitude of the patient. They should take very seriously any complaints made by her, and notice if there are persons or conditions she doesn't wish to talk about. They should note any marks or sores on her body, as well as missing clothing or other items.

Finances—Another Look

Earlier, in a list directed at the new retiree, I made a number of suggestions about saving money. These are just as valuable, when you're entering an assisted-living or nursing facility, as they ever were. Still, I believe you should re-think the matter.

Your expenses will increase, maybe sharply, at this juncture. But your lifestyle will change at the same time, so a look is in order.

You may not eat out so much, and probably you no longer drive, so some of the restaurant and shopping outlay can be reduced.

If you've quit driving, you'll be saving a lot of automobile expenses.

A simpler lifestyle may very well lead to fewer opportunities to wear expensive outfits.

Three meals a day will be provided—their cost being part of your higher expenses. But the supermarket will take much less of your money—both for lack of need and lack of opportunity.

You have to re-plan your financial future (or get help doing so) when you consider assisted living or a nursing home. You need to re-take the steps I earlier suggested, and re-calculate your expected income and expenses. The suggestions I made in Chapter 6 are still valid and should be reviewed.

All this might sound discouraging—a more limited life, higher expenses, and the need to consider how long you still have, and of course, it is. But, it has its upside, too. You can still arrange for family get-togethers, and you'll find yourself getting closer to the people who share your facilities. Also, your long experience with retirement makes it easier for you to estimate future financial needs. It's important, though, that you do this—even if (and especially if!) you hadn't reviewed such matters for some time.

CHAPTER 29

Mental Decline

Courage!

Not all mental issues result in dementia, and not all are serious. Nonetheless, almost every one experiencing forgetfulness or other mental slips asks himself if this could be the first sign of Alzheimer's. It usually isn't, and I'll comment on minor matters before I consider anything major.

All of you are likely to notice one or both of two developments: lowered ability to concentrate and lapses of memory. I've prepared two lists, with suggestions for each of these. Also, I'd like to make one or two comments here.

Both are part of the normal aging process. I'm not sure why we seem to have more trouble concentrating than we used to. But, it happens. It may have something to do with living less intensely after we retire, without as much need for high-powered thought. This might allow our brain to get a little sluggish.

Or, it might have something to do with our not having as many areas about which we care deeply as we used to. (Possibly, these two explanations amount to the same thing.) In any event, we do have some problems in concentrating. It shouldn't cause us concern, except perhaps when we're driving.

Memory lapses are also quite common, and I don't know anyone who hasn't experienced one. Indeed, most of us started noticing them long before we reached retirement age. One possible explanation is the ever-increasing amount of information we commit to memory over the years. It would not be surprising if available memory space becomes crowded.

However, more important that any of this, and one of the saddest developments in the aging process is the onset of mental deterioration. Watching a loved one suffer the ravages of memory loss and failing cognitive ability is devastating for those who care for him.

What can I say about this? What can anyone say? All one can do is express loving support for those caught up in the event. I lived through this for several years, and speak from firsthand experience.

In spite of research efforts, little is understood about the cause, and even the early detection, of such mental decline. There's no certain way to predict or prevent it, or stop it in its course. In brief, it's a disaster, and justifiably the most feared outcome of old age.

Some suggestions have been made. Many persons believe a healthy diet may deter the onset of Alzheimer's and similar dementia. It's also been advanced that the more actively one uses one's mind, the less likely one is to suffer mental loss, or defer it as long as possible. Some believe that regular physical activity will help.

There doesn't seem to be proof of any of these, but since all are of value for other reasons, it would seem desirable to practice such habits. I'm not going to say more about dementia, since I've already told virtually all I know, Instead, I'm going to add a few comments about dealing with it.

The first and foremost is to get help, if you're responsible for some one who's showing signs of dementia. Again, I speak from experience. In addition to the desolation of seeing an individual go from a sentient human being to a near-vegetable, there's the endless need for care, the everyday-ness of the demands of the illness, and the stress of being constantly on call—constantly worrying if you're doing the right thing.

All the above call for the care-giver to think of himself—to insure against becoming useless by breaking down and needing help too. The care-giver must take regular time off, and get supportive help from others. The Alzheimer's Association has support groups in every major community, and these are invaluable. In them, care-givers join with advisors to share experiences, problems, and learnings.

I've discussed earlier the existence of organizations providing in-home care. There's no circumstance where this is more critically needed than dealing with a person with dementia. Needless to say, the illness is expensive, and if money is a problem, it becomes urgent to find loving, volunteer assistance.

I mention the stress of not knowing you're doing the right thing. Since the disease is so little understand, everything that's tried is tried with a grain of salt. Somewhat like the anguish which first-time parents feel when their baby has a problem, and nothing they do helps, the care-giver in this case struggles with the same indecision and worry—but without the knowledgeable help new fathers and mothers get from professionals and experienced parents. Nor is there the hope for a brighter future. Instead, the sad prospect is for more decline, and an inevitable end.

I know all this sounds gloomy. And of course it is. It's dismal for any one undergoing mental decline, and for all those who care and help. The condition is alleviated somewhat by the fact that most persons suffering from it are not fully aware of what's happening. For the others, who, like President Reagan, face this unknown with dignity and courage, I have nothing but the greatest admiration.

In the following lists, I offer a few suggestions.

Concentration

One of the side effects (or maybe 'inside' effects) noticed by persons getting older is that it's not as easy to concentrate on any one thing for a long period of time as it used to be.

One place you'll notice this is when you're driving. I've already mentioned this in connection with that topic. But long familiarity with managing a car and coping with traffic makes it easy for your attention to wander—to what's visible off the road, to errands you're planning, or to other random thoughts.

The first step in dealing with this development is to notice it. As with other changes that occur gradually, diminished concentration escapes your attention until something forces you to notice. Let's hope it's not a car accident, a bad fall, or some other equally disturbing event.

Perhaps these words will serve to bring the matter to your attention.

Once you've noticed, you should do something. One thing is to have a means of reminding yourself to stay on target— whether this be a posted sign, an awkwardly-placed wrist watch, a timer, or a companion's reminder, doesn't matter.

All it needs to be is something that works for you—something which will call to your attention—at some kind of interval, or in some kind of circumstance—that you're supposed to be concentrating on a particular task, and DON'T FORGET IT!

You must get into the habit of noticing when your attention wanders, and under what conditions. Then, when these recur, you re-double your effort to pay attention to what you're doing.

I'm not sure loss of concentration is caused by the aging process so much as it might be due to lazy habits of thinking and living which we can get into as we get older. In other words, everything I discuss in other lists might be relevant.

Memory Loss

Memory loss and lowered concentration are in the same ballpark—both tell us something in our mind needs attention.

This something is not serious (true mental decline is considered later). But we all feel that anything in our mind that doesn't work exactly as we want it to is a concern.

The first problem most of us notice is short-term memory loss—we can't remember what we went into the kitchen for, we look up a telephone number, and lose it by the time we get to the phone, (or a myriad of other incidents). Efforts to recall familiar numbers, names, or objects founder on memory blanks.

The most obvious thing to do about this is make lists. As a matter of fact, if you ask almost any group of old people, you'll find everybody has a list—unless he forgot to bring it.

Another practice is to make associations—some people try to remember names by visualizing each person's face as they look at his name on a list, or they try to make mnemonic devices, like using words with the same initial letters to recall a number, or make a sentence out of words with the same initial letters as the words they want to remember.

Orderliness is another way to combat memory loss. If you have a system for arranging things you want to remember, you have a better chance of bringing them to mind. I suggest some ways to do this on the page which follows.

Memory triggers are used by many people, like a rubber band around your wrist, a ring on the wrong finger, a book placed upright on a table, or similar devices. These sometimes don't work too well, as they remind you to remember something, but don't say what. They should be combined with initial-letter help or some other mnemonic tool.

Memory Tips

This list carries on from the preceding one, to give illustrations of the devices I presented there.

An example of using initial letters to make numbers into names: for remembering 'sixty-two.' Try '<u>S</u>unday <u>t</u>rip' or '<u>s</u>cholarly <u>tw</u>in'; for 'sixty-three', try '<u>s</u>econd <u>th</u>ought' or '<u>s</u>he's <u>th</u>irsty.' You'll notice that if two or more numbers start with the same letter, you might use the first two (or three) letters in making a memory device.

For heaven's sake, don't use my concoctions—make your own, using words that have meaning for you.

Look at the list: '<u>b</u>read, <u>e</u>ggs, <u>m</u>eat, <u>l</u>ettuce, <u>c</u>orn <u>f</u>lakes'; this could become '<u>B</u>oys <u>e</u>njoy <u>m</u>ost <u>l</u>eftover <u>c</u>ooked-<u>f</u>oods' or '<u>B</u>ring <u>e</u>xtra <u>m</u>ayonnaise <u>l</u>ater; <u>c</u>ome-<u>f</u>ortified.' (You'll notice I used a hyphenated combination to represent a two-word item on the list.) You can re-arrange the words on the list to fit a different sentence structure; and if your sentence is senseless, ludicrous, or even untruthful, so much the better—it will be easier to remember.

It can even be a kind of recreation—you can have fun making up combinations of words. I just did, making up the ones above.

My last illustration is that of making a list orderly; suppose the list is 'grocery, drugstore, gasoline, shoes, dentist.' One simple way to organize is alphabetical: 'dentist, drugstore, gasoline, grocery, shoes.' Another is by the number of letters in each item: 'shoes, dentist, grocery, gasoline, drugstore' (two items have 7 letters each; I made them alphabetical). A third way is to calculate an efficient itinerary to do them all, and list them in the same order as you plan to travel. You can also list them in their order of importance, or urgency, or the best time for each. There's no end to the possibilities.

Remember to remember! Use the above, or create your own devices.

Dealing with Mental Decline

There are support groups widely available—use them! They provide opportunities to share your thoughts, feelings, experiences, and efforts—both successful and unsuccessful—with others in the same position, and they with you.

If you're the care-giver, Get help! Get help! Get help!

If you plan to use the services of an organization which provides in-home assistance, interview several, and, especially, talk with persons using any you're seriously considering.

You probably need to solicit help from family members and friends, particularly if you can't afford paid in-home assistance.

A resource to look into is a day-care facility specifically designed to care for persons with dementia (I used one affiliated with a local hospital). This is one way a care-giver can get some relief time.

The care-giver must arrange time for relief and re-charging.

There are many experimental programs around the country, testing various treatments. Try to get the patient into one. If you can, the people there will help you monitor changes in his condition, and give you information and advice.

The Alzheimer's Association has lots of useful materials available, to help you understand mental decline, and give ideas for care.

If the disabled person has a tendency to roam, the very least you can do is attach name, address, and contact information in some manner the patient cannot remove. Even better is an electronic device showing his position when away from home.

Sometimes, the individual can become aggressive, even dangerously so. If this occurs, home care is no longer feasible, and a locked professional facility will be needed.

CHAPTER 30

Leaving Your Affairs in Order
Giving to Your Family

Now we're really getting down to the end of the line, aren't we?

It seems a shame to talk about leaving your affairs in order when our whole emphasis has been on living to be 100. Still, it's only common-sense to realize that, 100 or not, we all have to go some time, and when we do, it's better to leave things as easy as possible for family members who survive.

I hate to repeat the advice you've received from so many sources so many times. Unfortunately, though, not all of you have followed that advice, so I'll lay mine on you, too. Though I fear you may not follow mine, either.

However, I'll try. First, be sure to make a will!!! Do it!—even if your estate is small and simple. Do it—even if you've received lots of advice about avoiding probate, and using trusts. It's a guaranteed way to be certain your wishes will be carried out as you want them to be, And the simpler your affairs are, the more you should avoid complicating them, as much advice to use trusts will do. I'm obviously not a lawyer, but I've received a lot of legal counsel from those who are, and it has been largely to this effect.

Just remember, too, that although it's possible a will you create yourself, without legal help, might stand up in court, it might not, either. So, don't try to write one, or use one of the canned forms so widely available. It's too easy to make a mistake, to be ambiguous, or do something you didn't intend, because you didn't know the law. Get the help of an attorney, and do it right. It shouldn't cost much if your estate is small; and if it's large, the expense is certainly justified.

You may well ask: "If you're not an attorney, how can you be qualified to give a legal opinion?" And you'll be right—I'm not. What I'm really doing is telling you the professional advice I received, and why. You should get your own advice from an attorney, in which case I think you'll be doing what I suggest.

But, leaving your affairs in order is not limited to making a will. There are many items you might like to dispose of which do not rise to the value and importance of being named in a legal document. You have a lot of personal possessions, and you may want to make sure certain people get certain things.

To do this, you can prepare a memorandum of your wishes, and leave it with your will, to guide your personal representative. Or, it can be left with someone else (assuming your inheritors get along well), who you know will carry out your wishes. Technically, such an item is not a legal document, and in the case of a disagreement would not prevail against the decisions of a person charged with carrying out the terms of the your will. So, you may wish to leave it for your personal representative, who I assume is someone you trust.

Your will, your instructions, and details of your financial affairs should not be kept in a safe-deposit box. Or if you feel better with them there, be sure to have photocopies of everything in a more convenient location. The main reason for this is that access to a safe-deposit box held in the name of a deceased person is blocked by the IRS until released.

I speak of "a more convenient location." To be specific, I not only refer to a location, but also to an orderly arrangement. Somewhere, which must be made known in advance to whomever is handling your estate, there should be a listing of such items as numbers and addresses for credit cards, bank accounts, outstanding loans, safe-deposit boxes, insurance policies, stock holdings, and other possessions and obligations—in short, everything your personal representative will need to do his job. All this should be carefully assembled, and reviewed each time there's a material change. You should also make sure the representative knows where everything is.

It's amazing how many people don't do what I've just suggested. From my own experience, I've seen estate executors desperately rummaging through desks and drawers and boxes to find what they need, and other family members sorting through the impedimenta of a household, asking why so much was kept—boxes of unsorted photos, lots of old correspondence, piles of outdated magazines, clothes which hadn't been worn for years, drawers full of junk, and cupboards full of clutter. It's almost as though the deceased party is punishing his family for having the unmitigated gall to outlive him.

On the next pages, I'm going to list the salient points of this discussion, and add a few other suggestions

Leaving Your Affairs in Order

Make a will!

Leave instructions for disposing of those possessions which are not included in your will.

I believe in letting everybody know in advance what's in your will. Why should it be a secret? Give your inheritors a chance to let you know if they think something is unfair. This is discussed in some detail in the next list.

If your family members get along well, you can leave more of the decisions to them. If they might have difficulty distributing items, especially those of sentimental value, discuss your possessions with them, decide who might best receive what, then make your instructions quite specific.

If certain possessions are particularly valuable, or are otherwise difficult to allocate on an equitable basis, you might leave an instruction to sell them, and add the proceeds to your estate. If later, the family wants to do it differently, and can agree on a procedure, there's no reason why this can't then be done then. In the ensuing list, I present a way of doing this.

Make copies of any important items that are kept in your safe-deposit box, and put them in a convenient location.

Assemble all salient information about your assets and liabilities, and keep it readily available for your personal representative.

Go through the clutter of your home—closets, cupboards, drawers, boxes, and piles—and throw out or give away anything you're not going to use in the near future. If any family member is interested in what's there, she can help. If there are items you think any one might care about, you can circulate a memo.

Planning with Your Family

Managing an inheritance is difficult—not only is the question of fairness involved, but the relationship of the various heirs with one another, and with you, can complicate matters.

In addition, there is the division of possessions which do not rise to the point of requiring treatment in the will. Often there are many unique or uniquely significant items which mean more to some persons than to others.

You should find out what things any family member particularly value, so that you can leave instructions to your personal representative, or, if needed, can include a clause in the will.

Discuss with your family how you think things should be handled after you're gone, so everyone can make requests and suggestions, or ask questions, and so all will know your thoughts. Identify issues before you pass on.

If any heirs desire one or more particularly desirable items, one solution is to find the items' value, add this amount to the estate, and then divide the resulting figure appropriately among the heirs, with anyone who gets a special allotment having it counted toward his share.

If relationships are friendly and easy, you can discuss the various possibilities with every one, perhaps in meetings with as many heirs as possible. Usually, an agreement can be reached, ensuring that no one will be unpleasantly surprised later.

If some strained relationships exist, at least you should make your decisions in as fair a manner as you can devise, and then explain yourself to your heirs in advance.

In the rare case where severe differences and/or possible litigation are present, early consultation gives everyone notice of difficulties ahead, and enables them to prepare themselves.

Planning with Professionals

For heaven's sake, have a lawyer prepare your will! For most estates the charge is not large. Don't use a pre-printed form. There are too many ways you can slip up and leave a will that's not valid, or doesn't do what you want it to. If you want to be sure your wishes prevail, use a lawyer,

Don't pay attention to the ads pushing a life trust, or some other way of avoiding probate. For all modest estates probate is not difficult, time-consuming, or costly. Further, if you forget to include something in a trust, even a trifle, the will may be subject to probate anyway.

For the vast majority of people, inheritance tax is not a problem. However, tax laws change, and few of us know their details. Again, I say that it's worthwhile to consult an accountant or attorney, specializing in wills and estates, to make sure that any liability is minimized or eliminated.

If, for any reason you wish to restrict any heir's inheritance, such as putting it in trust, or reducing it compared to others with a similar claim, it's essential you have professional assistance. It is in such cases that challenges and litigation occur. You need to be certain that your decisions are legally defensible.

Many components of an estate, such as IRA's, life insurance, joint ownership, and pensions, may have their own built-in procedures for transferring ownership upon the decease of the primary holder. Sometimes, past events have caused these no longer to reflect your intentions. The use of a competent professional can prevent anything going to the wrong person.

I don't mean to suggest that lawyers, accountants, investment advisors, and the like should be a regular part of your life. But if any of the possibilities I've mentioned are relevant to you, you may find the cost-benefit ratio of their counsel is indeed positive.

CHAPTER 31

Facing the Unknown

Peace and Hope

What can I say about this which will be helpful? We all have to face the unknown eventually, and we find many ways to do it. Nothing I say will really influence your feelings or beliefs.

Still, I want to present a few thoughts, though I'll give no hint about my own views. I don't think it's my job to proselytize, or say anything that challenges your beliefs. I hope in this way that you'll read my words with an open mind, without any pre-conceptions based on what I believe. Everyone has his own position—both what he believes, and what he thinks of the beliefs of others.

The first thing to say is that those who are serenely confident of the truth of their faith can face the future without fear, and deal with the present with equanimity. For them, they're not facing the unknown—they know what they face. And, it may well be that people with deep-seated religious beliefs tend to be happier and live longer than others.

You'll notice that I say 'serenely confident.' I do this because I notice that many persons seem to have a disconnect between what they profess to believe, and what they reveal in their everyday life. The individual who truly believes is one who practices what he professes, and shows his faith in his daily deeds.

The great works of all religions contain many statements about how the faithful should act. Some of these comments are extreme, and there are those who take one or more extreme statements, and base actions on them. The serene believer does not do this. Instead, he follows the precepts of the Bible or other religious writing in such a way as to reflect the central position it espouses.

There are many persons who do not adhere to a specific religion. Either agnostic or atheist, such people do not have a great book on which to base a faith. They may admire or respect such volumes, and may affirm much of what they contain. Still, they gain their view of life and death elsewhere.

Many such persons are fine people with a loving approach to humanity. Perhaps, it's this faith in his fellow-humans which provides the non-believer with the emotional stability to face the unknown. I've said elsewhere that all we have in this world is each other; and we draw great joy from human interaction. For atheists and agnostics, the present world is paramount, and the presence of others is both a challenge and a comfort.

All in all, one's deeply-held beliefs are central to one's peace of mind, especially as one gets older, and increasingly faces one's mortality. This peace of mind is crucial to the kind of lifestyle which can lead to an advanced old age.

For my readers with a profound religious faith, I urge you to do your best to live by it and through it—for both your own well-being and that of others. For non-believers, I urge them to reach out to other people in every way possible—to gain the serenity needed to face the unknown. For both, I would say that it's a terrible thing to face the final curtain with the feeling that one has left a lot of unfinished business behind.

I'll finish this chapter by noting that I've appended a section on hospice care. Perhaps it doesn't belong here—in a discussion of the unknown—but where else would I put it? It needs attention, since it's of critical value in an end-of-life situation. And it can be a major contributor to the peace of mind of every one involved. The hospice is such a wonderful development that I must say something about it.

Peace of Mind

This is a difficult area to deal with, involving, as it does, your religious faith. For persons with deeply-held religious beliefs, one of the great benefits they derive is peace of mind—feeling assured of a life hereafter, and having no doubt about how this present life should be lived.

Of course, peace of mind has additional elements than religion. It can reflect the knowledge that you have effectively met the challenges of life—success in marriage and child-rearing, achievement of career goals, and life as a good citizen, neighbor, and friend. For the faithful, it's also the cherished hope that they've lived up to the tenets of their religion.

However, some believers hold the conviction that they are lost in sin—they engage in constant self-flagellation. They give themselves little credit for the many good things they do. This surely fails to result in peace of mind.

I've seen that the faithful who evidence the greatest peace of mind are those who, in addition to religious observance, reach out to other people, and offer them help. As I've said before, we should do things of value to others. Probably, this is a key contributor to peace of mind.

Yet, few people are convinced they've lived up to all their hopes and aspirations. We all harbor unforgettable memories of times when we fell short, and did, or failed to do, something which causes us regret each time we think of it.

Nothing can erase the past, but the better a person you think you are today, the better you'll be able to handle the past. One of my reasons for writing this book is to present ideas on how to live, not only to 100 years of age, but also in such a way that it will reduce your self-doubt and self-criticism, help you come to terms with the past, and increase the likelihood that your feelings about yourself today will lead you to peace of mind.

Spirituality

The previous list dances around the question of human spirituality.

But all persons possess spirituality. It is that part of a human being that questions the purpose of life, asks how we came to be here, and where we're headed after life.

'Spirituality' is a word which is seldom present in the average person's conversation, or perhaps even in his thoughts. It seems too esoteric to many, and too distant from the concerns of everyday life.

For religious followers, their beliefs <u>are</u> their spirituality. They hear the word in church or mosque or synagogue, and in serious talk about their faith.

But for everyone else, it's a concept which is hard to come to terms with.

I suggest that it should not be this way. Especially for the aging retiree, thought should be given to the mystery of life. As you get older, the realization of your mortality becomes more intense, so what else is more important to do than reflect on it, and try to come to terms with it?

One of the problems of old age is the shallowness of conversation one hears in senior centers and retirement homes. Older people have fewer opportunities to experience challenging ideas and events in their lives, so there's endless talk about the weather, their families, their aches and pains, their past lives, and the current gossip.

I believe we deserve better than this, and I urge you to do at least occasional reading on spiritual matters, and exchange thoughts with your friends. I've found that the days when I do this, I go to bed that night in a calmer and more relaxed frame of mind.

Religious Beliefs

In a book such as this, it would not be proper for me to proselytize, or even reveal my own beliefs. Still, the area of religion is so important to so many people, especially as they age, that the topic must be part of it.

Writing about religious beliefs is a real challenge, since one's audience ranges from devout believers, through those with varying degrees of intensity in their faith, to agnostics and atheists. I would like to say something helpful to everyone, without offending anybody by seeming to slight their beliefs.

All great religions espouse love, charity, and tolerance—as expressed in their great books. And surely these precepts also resonate with those persons who don't accept religion. They are implicit in much of the advice I advance in this book

Perhaps the people who berate themselves for sinfulness should grant themselves the same charity they seek to grant others, and give themselves credit for trying hard and being faithful.

"Love they neighbor as thyself" might have appended to it, "and love thyself as thy neighbor."

I've had many agnostic or atheistic friends who practice love, charity, and tolerance, and possess great peace of mind. You may wonder how persons with no conviction of an afterlife can avoid depression and sadness when they believe the present world is all they have.

Apparently, for them, as well as for believers, the importance of human beings—the crucial significance of those who co-inhabit the world with us—is a great motivator. It would seem that the calm demeanor of many non-religious friends is clear evidence of this.

For those of you with the conviction of a guaranteed afterlife, I say you are indeed fortunate, and you need no advice from me.

Hospice Care

In spite of the gloomy thought that hospice care is for some one in the last stages of life, the practice is one of the best achievements of our time.

Often in the past, the terminally-ill patient spent his final days in a sterile hospital room, tied to needles, tubes and machines, tended to by busy professionals, and with no convenient place for his family to be with him.

The hospice is conceived as an alternative to all that. Once it's determined that the patient is not going to recover, he's transferred to a location where everything is arranged for his comfort and care, and for facilitating visits by his family. This can contribute to his peace of mind at a critical juncture.

The location is usually in the hospice itself, which is not organized for the treatment of illness, but for making the patient as comfortable as possible, easing any pain he suffers, and furnishing TLC generously.

But hospice care may not be in the hospice building itself. It can be in a nursing facility, or in the patient's own home. In such a case there will be regular visits from specially-trained hospice personnel, who not only insure the patient is getting the best care possible, but also help the family with their own needs in a difficult time.

And when the end comes, the hospice people are there to assist with necessary arrangements, and provide or find counseling for anyone who needs it.

I consider hospice workers to be special! If you need to use them, you'll find them to be special too!

Epilog:
Last Word

I've Done My Best

What is there to say at the end of a book that hasn't already been said in it?

Probably nothing—if the final remarks are to be at all relevant. Perhaps, too, you think, and maybe I do too, that I really said my last word in the last chapter.

Yet, it's customary to leave readers with a message which in some way sums up all that's gone before.

So, I'll try.

But, before I do, I'll add a few words about my own trials during the production of this little volume. I never realized, when I started on it, the extent to which my suggestions would be put to the test on myself.

I've already reported that I suffered a stroke a few months ago and that I'm trying to recover my strength and capabilities. I'll now remark that I've learned how hard it is to do some of the actions I've proposed to you. I've found how much willpower is needed when you're in pain, or desperately weary, to do what you're supposed to do. I've also found how easy it is to backslide, or to rationalize skipping something. I confess that all this occurred.

However, when I had a chance to reflect on my shortcomings, I came to the conclusion that if I felt strongly enough about the things I'm saying to put them in a book, they must be worth an extra effort on my part. So, I'm reporting that I've done my best to apply to myself the precepts I'm asking you to apply to yourself. Although not all the results are in, the preliminary outcomes are favorable. In particular, I tried to follow my own suggestions, especially in areas related to health care and relations with other people, and I found that when I did so, I felt better. I felt better in that I felt good about doing the difficult thing, but I also felt better physically. I think I can say that at least some of the points I've made in this book do work.

And now, I'll go back to my intention to write a last word.

Basically, from start to finish, I've been saying that if you want to live to be 100, you should apply certain principles, which I've stressed throughout, and which I won't repeat at this time (although maybe in the ensuing list).

I shall note, however, that since no one is perfect, you may not be able to follow these faultlessly. (And you may not even wish to.) Also, since the not-perfect group certainly includes myself, there's even the faint possibility that my principles might not be infallible, and you (or I) might not get to be 100.

So, if you don't reach 100, try not to blame me, and I'll try not to blame you. It could be the fault of either or both of us—or neither. But, if you want to register a complaint with me for failing to become a centenarian, be sure to give me a return address, so that I can reply.

Seriously, though, I've written this little handbook to share what I've learned in the years since I retired in 1974. Also, I'm trying to refute the widely held opinion that no one past 65 knows much of anything, and most of what he does know is passé.

Finally, I'd like to express the hope that some day the U.S. will adopt the practice of some older civilizations, and honor and solicit the wisdom of elders. Please join me in this quest, and take it on yourself to make your retirement years meaningful both to yourself, and to the younger generations who need your wisdom—even if they don't know it.
As always, I'll append a list.

Last Thoughts

A Summing Up

Retirement is a new life—all the rest of your life.

It should be planned for, both at the outset, and on a regular basis, and especially when conditions change.

It has several stages, ranging from the early days, through the active years, the later years, and on—as long as you live.

If you want to be alive at 100, the acronym, A.L.I.V.E., points the way:

<u>A</u>ctivity	Make both physical and mental activity a part of every day.
<u>L</u>ooking Ahead	Always have some event in prospect.
<u>I</u>ndependence	Take charge of your life, and do for yourself as much as possible.
Being of <u>V</u>alue	Do things for others that they will value.
<u>E</u>mpathy	Show sensitivity for others' feelings, and interact with them frequently.

Then, do all that in the manner of the 4 U's:

Understanding of Self

Understanding of Others

Upbeat-ness

Un-Rigidity

And if you do it all as I have proposed, you'll have done everything I think will help you get to be 100—and happy. You'll have done more than I've been able to do—yet. And you'll be an inspiration to everyone!

GOODBYE AND GOOD LUCK!

Afterword

Now the book is finished, and in a few days will go to the publisher. It is October, 2010, and I feel I should report my experiences since my stroke Since it clearly affects my enjoyment of life, it consequently brings into question my efforts to help you do the same.

I've commented on various consequences of this stroke in the body of the text. I shall now summarize my present circumstances.

I still suffer some debility. I still don't drive. I still walk with a cane. I'm still taking physical and speech therapy. I was forced to give away my dog.

Still, my frame of mind is upbeat. I've hired a young man to drive me around in my car so that I can shop, do errands, make appointments, and take rides. I do 18 exercises and walk a mile every day, to try to regain strength in my right arm and leg. And I hope soon to enroll in a special training program to enable me to drive again.

No one knows what the future will bring, and no one is able to give me any assurances. But I'm optimistic. I keep myself busy, using my word processor one to two hours a day, writing children's stories, as well as readying this book for publication.

I get out of my residence every day that the weather permits, even if it's only a walk to a nearby supermarket. I eat out at a restaurant at least three times a week. In short, I'm doing everything I can to live a life that's as normal as possible.

I know I'm at an increased risk of another stroke, and am taking medicine to reduce that likelihood, I may not live to be 100 (I'm 94), but if not, I'm certainly going to "die trying."

I still enjoy life! I hope you do the same.